NEW VANGUARD 311

US NAVY ARMORED CRUISERS 1890–1933

BRIAN LANE HERDER   ILLUSTRATED BY PAUL WRIGHT

OSPREY PUBLISHING
Bloomsbury Publishing Plc
Kemp House, Chawley Park, Cumnor Hill, Oxford OX2 9PH, UK
29 Earlsfort Terrace, Dublin 2, Ireland
1385 Broadway, 5th Floor, New York, NY 10018, USA
E-mail: info@ospreypublishing.com
www.ospreypublishing.com

OSPREY is a trademark of Osprey Publishing Ltd

First published in Great Britain in 2022

A catalog record for this book is available from the British Library.

ISBN: PB 9781472851000; eBook: 9781472851017;
ePDF 9781472851024; XML: 9781472851062

22 23 24 25 26 10 9 8 7 6 5 4 3 2 1

Index by Angela Hall
Typeset by PDQ Digital Media Solutions, Bungay, UK
Printed and bound in India by Replika Press Private Ltd.

Osprey Publishing supports the Woodland Trust, the UK's leading woodland
conservation charity.

To find out more about our authors and books visit
www.ospreypublishing.com. Here you will find extracts, author
interviews, details of forthcoming events and the option to sign up for our
newsletter.

CONTENTS

US NAVY ARMORED CRUISERS 1890–1933

INTRODUCTION

Armored cruisers are likely the most controversial major ship type in modern naval history. Despite being as large and expensive as contemporary battleships, armored cruisers could not withstand a battleship in combat. Instead, an armored cruiser's strengths were high speed and long range. But, as even contemporary strategists pointed out, naval wars are rarely won by running away from more powerful ships.

Not including the re-designated 1895 battleship *Maine*, the United States Navy (USN) commissioned 12 true armored cruisers between 1893 and 1908. The first two, *New York* and *Brooklyn*, were commissioned in 1893 and 1896 respectively and saw heavy action in the 1898 Spanish-American War. They were followed in 1905–08 by the six Pennsylvania- and four Tennessee-class armored cruisers, plus three St. Louis-class "semi-armored" cruisers. In addition to World War I convoy duty, these post-1898 vessels engaged in frequent gunboat-type operations overseas, ultimately leading diverse careers that were often marked by strange and unfortunate luck.

Around 1909 the new battlecruiser type decisively made the armored cruiser obsolete – with its state-of-the-art turbine engines and large battleship guns, a battlecruiser could run down an armored cruiser and destroy it from outside the armored cruiser's effective gun range. All but one US armored cruiser had originally been named after states, as US law required of capital ships. However, between 1911 and 1920 the USN renamed all its state-named armored cruisers after cities, reflecting the type's fading status. In all cases the stripped state names were immediately reassigned to newly authorized dreadnought battleships.

An 1899 painting of the first two US Navy armored cruisers. In the foreground is USS *Brooklyn*. Her three funnels were 100ft tall to maximize induced draft. On the horizon to the left is USS *New York*. Like all future US armored cruisers, *Brooklyn* and *New York* were designed for high speed and long range, giving strategic mobility for flagship duty. (Getty Images 3202940)

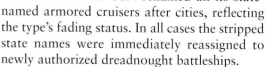

DESIGN AND DEVELOPMENT

By the 1870s, cruisers could no longer mount wrought iron armor thick enough to resist the era's continuously improving naval guns. In lieu of heavy side armor, new cruisers were fitted with only a thin turtleback steel deck extending below the waterline. This "protected deck" could only shield vulnerable machinery spaces from splinter damage and oblique hits. This new warship type became known as "protected" cruisers. However, armor plate technology soon advanced as well. Within a few years, the largest steel cruisers mounted not just a protective deck but could also be fitted with an additional armored belt to protect their waterline. Heavier and more robust than protected cruisers, these new warships became known as "armored" cruisers.

Second-class battleship and former armored cruiser *Maine* in New York, circa 1896. At 16.5kts, *Maine* was considerably slower than the new generation of armored cruisers, but with four 10in/30 guns and a 12in nickel steel belt, she was far better armed and protected. (LC-DIG-det-4a14340)

During the 1870s and 1880s, armored cruisers were effectively small, cut-rate battleships mounting relatively heavy firepower and armor protection. For major empires, such as Britain, armored cruisers were ideal for permanent deployment on backwater overseas stations, such as China. Compared to front-line battleships, armored cruisers were smaller and less expensive, and their shallower draft made them more suitable to steaming coastal waters and major rivers than full-fledged battleships. To second-class navies, armored cruisers functioned as prestigious front-line warships that were nevertheless more affordable than true battleships.

Concerned with countering the 5,029-ton Brazilian battleship *Riachuelo*, on August 3, 1886, the US Congress authorized a 6,000-ton armored cruiser and a 6,000-ton battleship; these became *Maine* and *Texas* respectively and were the USN's first steel-constructed capital ships. Incidentally, the period corresponded with a brief but intense fad for ramming tactics, which demanded end-on fire and suggested "line across" tactics or even one-on-one mêlées. *Maine* and *Texas* were accordingly designed with a *Riachuelo*-style "echeloned" battery arrangement, which theoretically allowed all heavy guns to fire in any direction.

During the 1880s a newly revitalized US Navy began to shift doctrine towards "sea control," an offensive strategy that stressed a concentrated fleet of first-class battleships. Although he did not invent the concept, the new strategy became most associated with a USN professor named Alfred Thayer Mahan. By 1890 the new Secretary of the Navy, Benjamin F. Tracy, would wholeheartedly adopt Mahan's theories stressing a concentrated fleet of purely first-class battleships, precipitating a change in US cruiser theory. The original armored cruiser idea, really a scaled-down battleship, was discarded, and none past *Maine* would be built.

Additionally, by 1892 new French and British rapid-firing 6in guns would abruptly discredit ramming tactics, rendering *Maine*'s echeloned battery arrangement obsolete. Despite mounting four 10in guns, *Maine* now clearly lacked the firepower or protection to fight a modern first-class battleship, while her performance fell short of new armored cruiser designs. While *Maine* was still under construction, the USN accordingly reclassified both she and her half-sister *Texas* as "Second-Class Battleships," a term introduced by the Royal Navy in 1890.

Maine was finally commissioned in 1895 but was denied the honor of being the USN's first official armored cruiser. Just three years later, on

February 15, 1898, *Maine* would be destroyed at Havana by a mysterious explosion. Ironically, in 1920 the USN retroactively reclassified the long-gone *Maine* with her original "armored cruiser" status and gave her the hull designator ACR-1 (Armored Cruiser No. 1).[1]

Subsequent US armored cruisers (like their foreign counterparts) would be fast, long-ranged, and designed for deep-sea operations. Armored cruisers' firepower and protection, while still greater than that of protected cruisers, would now be clearly subordinated to performance. With their superior speed and range, armored cruisers would now complement the USN's planned first-class battleships, rather than supplement them.

Secretary Tracy ostensibly explained the purpose behind post-*Maine* US armored cruisers in his 1890 *Annual Report*. Referring to the USN's new armored cruiser *New York*, then under construction, Tracy announced: "She is built to keep the sea and thus destroy an enemy's commerce, and not only his commerce, but any commerce destroyer he may send out. For general purposes of service in war she is believed to have a wider field of usefulness than any other ship yet designed for the Navy."

US armored cruisers' higher speed and longer range compared to US battleships required higher freeboard for superior seakeeping, as well as a large size to house the powerful machinery and capacious coal bunkers required for increased performance. Additionally, their finer hull ratios increased power- and fuel-efficiency, aiding both speed and range. US armored cruisers therefore tended to be longer, narrower, and higher than contemporary US battleships. Such increased performance on a hull no larger or more expensive than a battleship came at a price, and this price was paid through substantially inferior firepower and protection. This was not a design flaw, but a conscious design decision inherent to all armored cruisers and unavoidable under the limitations of 1890s-era powerplants. It was this compromise, however, that ultimately made armored cruisers such

1   For further information on *Maine*, please see this author's NVG 271: *US Navy Battleships 1886–98*.

A

PRE-SPANISH-AMERICAN WAR

1. The USN's first armored cruiser, USS *New York* (ACR-2) appears above upon her August 1893 commissioning in the USN's then standard white hull and ocher superstructure. *New York* was immediately the USN's most plum assignment. She was first deployed to the South Atlantic Squadron, before being transferred to the North Atlantic Squadron for flagship duty in August 1894. *New York* was temporarily assigned as the European Squadron flagship in June 1895, so that the USN could be represented by its most modern and powerful warship at the opening of Germany's Kiel Canal. She then returned to the North Atlantic Squadron until the outbreak of the Spanish-American War in April 1898.

2. USS *Brooklyn* (ACR-3) appears below in 1897, just after her December 1896 commissioning under Captain F. A. Cook. Like *New York*, *Brooklyn* is also in the USN's peacetime 1890s livery. During *Brooklyn*'s sea trials, an official remarked: "The wonderful steadiness of the ship while being driven under forced draft was remarked by all on board. The fine lines of the hull were shown in the way the *Brooklyn* goes through the water when being speeded. There was no great bow wave, but the vessel threw the water to each side as cleanly as a knife cuts through cloth."

Brooklyn's first operational deployment was a diplomatic mission to Britain. On June 26, 1897, *Brooklyn* represented the United States for Queen Victoria's Diamond Jubilee Naval Review at Spithead. Ironically it was here that Charles Algernon Parsons bombastically raced his experimental *Turbinia* up and down the lines of warships at an unprecedented 34 knots. *Turbinia* was of course powered by Parsons' brand-new turbine engine, the technology that would shortly render armored cruisers obsolete at a stroke. *Brooklyn* departed Southampton on July 6, 1897 to return to the United States.

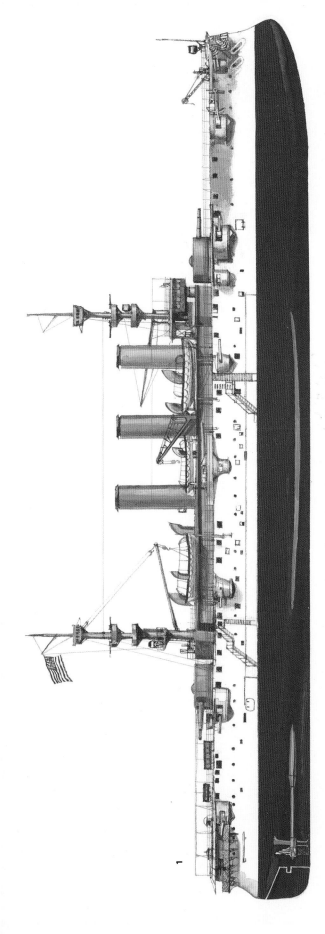

1

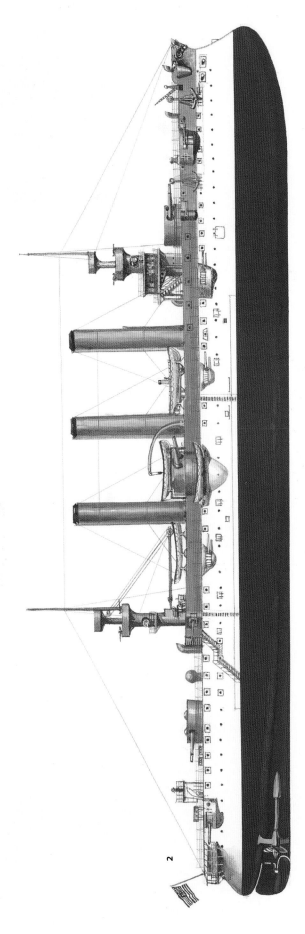

2

The *Tennessee*'s 10in/40 main guns fired a 510lb armor piercing shell at a muzzle velocity of 2,700ft per second, doubling the power of the Pennsylvania-class's 8in/40 guns. The 10in/40 was unique to the Tennessee-class and was the most powerful ever mounted aboard a US cruiser until 1944, when it was eclipsed by the Alaska-class' 12in/50. USS *Tennessee*'s forward 10in/40 turret is seen circa 1907–08. (NH 94013)

a controversial type in the first place. Indeed, as early as 1900 a future USN Chief Constructor observed: "The question at once arises whether it is worthwhile to continue to build armored cruisers inferior to battleships in so many respects and superior to them in so few."

Mahan himself believed "compromise" in warship design to be inherently negative. Around 1905 he explicitly denounced the armored cruiser, calling the type a "fad": "What have you got?... You have in her more cruiser than she ought to have and less armored vessel, or less cruiser and more armored ship ... I do not say that you have a useless ship. I say that you have not as useful a ship, as, for the tonnage, you ought to have."

The Pennsylvania-class illustrates the armored cruiser type's controversial, even schizophrenic reputation. In 1900 *Pennsylvania*'s designers had giddily imagined their creation challenging existing battleships. But within a few years the heady optimism had vanished. A 1908 issue of the Naval Institute's *Proceedings* stated:

> Take as a concrete example a battleship matched against an armored cruiser, as for instance the *Virginia* against the *Washington*. Here the displacements are nearly equal, the date is about the same, and as they were designed by the same board they may be assumed to be equally well designed. The latter is nothing in the world but a battleship where guns and armor have been sacrificed for three knots' speed. The broadside fire of the *Virginia* is four 12-inch, six 8-inch, and six 6-inch guns against four 10-inch and eight 6-inch in the *Washington*. We see it stated that the faster ship can regulate the range to suit herself. Can anyone hope so to regulate this range that the *Washington*'s battery can do more damage to her adversary's 11-inch belt and 6-inch side and diagonal armor than the *Virginia*'s can do to her opponent's 5-inch belt and side? The faster ship would probably be winged long before she got within range of her 6-inch battery.
>
> It is very doubtful if an armored cruiser of the [*Pennsylvania*-class] would ever tackle a monitor, for fear that one of the latter's shot *might* hit a vital spot, and if it did she would lose her only *raison d'être*, for a crippled cruiser would be useless as a cruiser, and still not fit to "lie in the line."... It may be argued that an armored cruiser was never intended to fight a battleship. Then what *is* she intended for? Surely not as a scout or commerce destroyer, for vessels a fifth the displacement could do this work as well, and numbers are required here, not strength... If she is to overtake a weaker enemy, you must first assume a smaller enemy, otherwise she could not have superiority in both speed and strength. By escaping from a stronger enemy she will never win wars.

Indeed, by 1908 the "capital ship" concept had become quite messy, with four separate types crowding the term. Of these, the armored cruiser's validity had become the most dubious. Confirmation of the armored cruiser's obsolescence came on December 8, 1914, when British battlecruisers

Invincible and *Inflexible* battered the relatively modern German armored cruisers *Scharnhorst* and *Gneisenau* into oblivion off the Falkland Islands. To US officers, the Falklands revealed that a modern *Invincible*-class battlecruiser "could destroy either a [*Tennessee*] or a [*Pennsylvania*] at extreme range without receiving enough punishment to note in the ship's log."

Tennessee-class and selected contemporaries (1910)

Navy	Type	Class	Tons	Belt	Main battery	Speed
USN	Armored cruiser	*Tennessee* (1906)	14,500	5in	Four 10in/40	22kts
RN	Armored cruiser	*Warrior* (1906)	12,600	6in	Six 9.2in/47	23kts
KM	Armored cruiser	*Scharnhorst* (1907)	12,985	5.9in	Eight 8.3in/40	23kts
IJN	Armored cruiser	*Tsukaba* (1907)	13,750	7.1in	Four 12in/45	20kts
RN	Battlecruiser	*Invincible* (1908)	17,250	6in	Eight 12in/45	25kts
USN	Pre-dreadnought	*Connecticut* (1906)	16,000	11in	Four 12in/45	19kts
RN	Dreadnought	*Dreadnought* (1906)	17,900	11in	Ten 12in/45	21kts
USN	Dreadnought	*South Carolina* (1910)	16,000	12in	Eight 12in/45	18kts

By 1909, US capital ships had begun undergoing major modernizations to correct deficiencies revealed by the 1907–09 "Great White Fleet" global cruise. Even before the battleships returned, the USN repainted its white-and-ocher armored cruisers with a permanent warlike haze gray. Over the next several years, strong and lightweight lattice foremasts replaced the armored cruisers' old, top-heavy military masts, and would mount modern new centralized fire control systems. Turret interiors were almost completely rebuilt for improved flash protection. Extraneous equipment and ornamentation were removed, and wireless transceivers (radio) installed. Additionally, the World War I U-boat peril caused the USN to remove most US armored cruisers' secondary guns to help arm US merchantmen. By 1918, US armored cruisers would also sport wartime "dazzle schemes" designed to confuse U-boats' ranging.

Classifications and naming

In 1891 the USN began assigning its warships type-specific hull numbers. For instance, in 1893 *New York* was commissioned "Armored Cruiser No. 2," often abbreviated to ACR-2. *Brooklyn* was "Armored Cruiser No. 3," or ACR-3, and so on. All remaining US cruisers were assigned a single hull-number series separate from armored cruisers; *St. Louis* for example was originally "Cruiser No. 20," typically abbreviated as C-20.

However, in July 1920, all US armored cruisers were reclassified as "First Line Cruisers" and given a new two-letter CA type hull designator, while keeping their original hull numbers. For example, Armored Cruiser *Brooklyn* (ACR-3) now became First Line Cruiser *Brooklyn* (CA-3). The surviving *St. Louis* and *Charleston* semi-armored cruisers were also reclassified as first line cruisers and renumbered within the

Outrun and outranged by British battlecruisers, the German armored cruiser *Scharnhorst* succumbs to withering British fire at the December 8, 1914, Battle of the Falkland Islands. Behind her, *Scharnhorst's* doomed sister-ship *Gneisenau* struggles on. Despite the British victory, battlecruisers were just 18 months from seeing their own reputation permanently destroyed at Jutland. (Author's collection)

USS *Huntington* (ex-*West Virginia*) catapults a Curtiss F seaplane from her stern-mounted catapult while underway off Pensacola, June 25, 1917. Although *Pennsylvania* conducted aviation experiments in 1911, her equipment was not permanent. After *North Carolina*, *Huntington* was the second US armored cruiser equipped with operational aviation facilities. (NH 44221-A)

same series (now CA-18 and CA-19 respectively). Then in August 1921, the first line cruisers were reclassified back to official armored cruisers but kept the CA hull designator. Finally, in July 1931 all surviving armored cruisers were reclassified as "heavy cruisers" (CA) and the armored cruiser officially ceased to exist.

US federal law had long required all "first class" US warships to be named after "the States of this Union." By the 1880s, "first class" obviously included the new steel battleships. Intriguingly, the USN also named its new armored cruisers after US states, while naming its smaller cruisers after American cities. Such conventions imply the USN originally considered its armored cruisers to be capital ships like battleships, with smaller cruisers classified as second-rate. However, in 1910 the USN began commissioning its first modern dreadnought battleships. These were far superior warships to the now obsolete armored cruisers. State names are intrinsically political, and the following year the USN began stripping state names from its existing armored cruisers and reassigning them to the newly authorized 14in-gunned "superdreadnought" battleships, beginning with *New York* (BB-34) in 1911.

When US armored cruisers were renamed, they were always renamed after cities or towns in their original eponymous state. *New York* was uniquely renamed twice – first to *Saratoga* in 1911, and then to *Rochester* in 1917. Because *Brooklyn* alone was originally named after a city, not a state, it was never renamed in deference to a newly authorized dreadnought, nor were the St. Louis-class semi-armored cruisers.

Cruiser		Commissioned	Second Name	Third Name
ACR-1	*Maine*	Sep 17, 1895	N/A	N/A
ACR-2/CA-2	*New York*	Aug 1, 1893	*Saratoga* Feb 16, 1911	*Rochester* Dec 1, 1917
ACR-3/CA-3	*Brooklyn*	Dec 1, 1896	N/A	N/A
ACR-4/CA-4	*Pennsylvania*	Mar 9, 1905	*Pittsburgh* Aug 27, 1912	N/A
ACR-5/CA-5	*West Virginia*	Feb 23, 1905	*Huntington* Nov 11, 1916	N/A
ACR-6/CA-6	*California*	Aug 1, 1907	*San Diego* Sep 1, 1914	N/A
ACR-7/CA-7	*Colorado*	Jan 19, 1905	*Pueblo* Nov 9, 1916	N/A
ACR-8/CA-8	*Maryland*	Apr 18, 1905	*Frederick* Nov 9, 1916	N/A
ACR-9/CA-9	*South Dakota*	Jan 27, 1908	*Huron* Jun 7, 1920	N/A
ACR-10/CA-10	*Tennessee*	Jul 17, 1906	*Memphis* May 26, 1916	N/A
ACR-11/CA-11	*Washington*	Aug 7, 1906	*Seattle* Nov 9, 1916	N/A
ACR-12/CA-12	*North Carolina*	May 7, 1908	*Charlotte* Jun 7, 1920	N/A
ACR-13/CA-13	*Montana*	Jul 21, 1908	*Missoula* Jun 7, 1920	N/A
C-20/CA-18	*St. Louis*	Aug 18, 1906	N/A	N/A
C-21	*Milwaukee*	Dec 10, 1906	N/A	N/A
C-22/CA-19	*Charleston*	Oct 17, 1905	N/A	N/A

Construction

All US armored cruisers were powered by vertical triple expansion (VTE) engines driving twin shafts. A VTE routed steam into an initial high-pressure cylinder, where it drove a piston attached to a crankshaft. The now lower pressure steam was then exhausted into a second, medium-pressure cylinder, whose larger piston size allowed it to extract additional energy. The process was then repeated a final time, with the steam routed to a third, even larger low-pressure cylinder, before the steam was finally exhausted for good. However, the Pennsylvania-, Tennessee-, and St. Louis-classes mounted four-cylinder VTEs, designed with dual low-pressure cylinders to reduce vibration.

US armored cruisers mounted an 8in or 10in (Tennessee-class) main battery along with a "rapid-firing" (RF) secondary battery for torpedo boat defense. Smaller-caliber tertiary batteries provided automatic fire against exposed enemy personnel. Although New York's and Brooklyn's guns were designed for brown (or "cocoa") powder propellant, in 1900 the USN introduced its superior "smokeless" powder propellant, based on the French Poudre B. Smokeless powder burned slower and smoother than brown powder. This allowed for a longer projectile acceleration time, which in turn demanded longer barrels. The resulting combination of longer, smoother acceleration and longer barrels significantly increased muzzle velocity, producing much greater range, accuracy, and hitting power than the previous generation of brown-powder weapons.

This revolutionary jump in gun power suddenly allowed new cruisers to mount cruiser-sized guns whose power rivaled those mounted on the existing, but now outdated, generation of battleships. This development briefly returned armored cruisers to favor, with the Pennsylvania-, Tennessee-, and St. Louis-class cruisers all designed from the beginning to mount smokeless powder-powered guns. New York and Brooklyn were later re-armed with smokeless powder guns during refits.

US armored cruisers also mounted torpedo tubes, whose efficacy and potential vulnerability to explosion were fiercely controversial. The standard 18in Whitehead torpedoes had a 1,500yd range, while the Tennessee-class's 21in Bliss-Leavitt torpedoes could reach 4,500yds.

Subdivided compartments, watertight bulkheads, and (largely ineffective) cellulose cofferdams provided US armored cruisers' underwater protection, which was nevertheless poor by modern standards. However, rapidly advancing armor plate technology allowed late 19th-century navies to devote less design weight to armor. By the 1890s, lighter, state-of-the-art Harvey and Krupp armor plate allowed armored cruisers to effectively transition roles from cumbersome second-class battleships to powerful, high-speed cruisers.

Armored cruiser Washington slides down the slipways at the New York Shipbuilding Company in Camden, New Jersey on March 18, 1905. Numerous rowboats (presumably civilians) are alongside to observe, while in the background on the right a tugboat appears ready to assist. (NH 50393)

Year	Armor type	Equivalent
1876	Mild steel	12in
1877	Compound	12in
1889	Nickel-steel	11.5in
1890	Harvey	7.5in
1893	Krupp	7in

The first armored cruisers 1893–96
USS *New York* (1893)

On September 9, 1888, Congress authorized the single largest warship construction program since the Civil War, totaling 27,436 tons. Among the seven cruisers authorized was "one armored cruiser of about 7,500 tons displacement, to cost, exclusive of armament, not more than $3,500,000." The original concept was an improved *Maine* that would mount two 12in guns. After further development, a four-gun 11in battery was approved in August 1889. Combined with an 11in armor belt, the new cruiser would effectively be a *Maine*-type second-class battleship.

However, by January 1890 Secretary Tracy had fully committed to a fleet of first-class battleships, making the *Maine*-style second-class battleship obsolete. A month later, the 1888 armored cruiser authorization had evolved into a completely new 8,100-ton "thinly-armored" fast cruiser design whose speed would be brought through a lighter battery and greatly depleted armor protection. Although still designated an "armored cruiser," this evolved design was in fact an entirely different warship intended for an entirely different mission.

New York was laid down at Philadelphia's William Cramp & Sons on September 20, 1890 and commissioned on August 1, 1893. *New York* was the USN's first armored ship to enter service. Upon commissioning, *New York* was the finest armored cruiser in the world, meaning she was also the Steel Navy's first ship that could claim to be the best example of its type.

New York's main battery comprised six 8in/35 guns. Four 8in/35s were mounted in two centerline twin turrets, one turret fore and one turret aft. The remaining two 8in/35 guns were mounted amidships in carriages and could be trained and elevated by hand only. In theory they could fire directly ahead and astern, but this was avoided in practice because of blast effects.

New York dressed out, probably in the Hudson River, April 1899. Intended for high-speed operations on the deep sea, her freeboard was considerably higher than US pre-dreadnought battleships designed at the same time. Upon commissioning, *New York* increased the total horsepower in the US fleet by 17 percent. (LC-DIG-det-4a14507)

However, when trained abeam, the amidship guns gave *New York* a heavy broadside of five 8in guns.

The era's standard European secondary battery caliber was the 6in RF gun. However, US federal law required US warships be constructed entirely in the United States, whose nascent ordnance industry still trailed Europe's by several years. *New York*'s secondary battery was thus restricted to 12 4in/40 RF guns, the largest caliber RF gun American industry could produce in 1893. Eight 6-pdrs, two 1-pdrs, and four .50-caliber Gatlings provided *New York*'s tertiary battery. *New York* additionally mounted three 18in Whitehead torpedo tubes.

The crew of *New York*'s forward main turret display their 8in/35 gun breech while posing for the camera, 1899. The 8in/35 fired a 260lb AP shell at a muzzle velocity of 2,100ft per second. The average 1890s firing rate was less than one round per minute; improved loading techniques doubled this by the early 1900s. (LC-DIG-DET-4a14528)

Although Harvey armor had just been invented, American armor production capacity was still limited. Priority went to battleships *Maine* and *Texas*, meaning *New York* was armored with standard nickel-steel. *New York* was fitted with a 200ft long, 4–5in thick waterline belt.

Six double-ended Fox fire-tube boilers provided steam to four 4,000hp VTE engines, with two VTEs per shaft for a combined 16,000hp. Three 80ft funnels maximized induced draft, allowing forced draft to be saved for combat and emergency conditions. At low speeds, the forward VTE on each shaft was designed to decouple, allowing *New York* to cruise on her two after VTEs only, for improved fuel efficiency. *New York* achieved 21.9 knots during trials, a new world record.

Secretary Tracy described *New York* as "An unusual combination of great offensive and defensive power, with extraordinary coal endurance, and a high rate of speed which is sufficient to enable her to escape from any more powerful ship afloat today, and to overtake the majority – certainly 95 percent – of all the ships in the world, naval or mercantile." Tracy even claimed *New York*'s firepower gave her "chances which are not to be despised should she be driven to a momentary encounter with a battleship," while admittedly noting, "Fighting battleships, however, is not her business."

In 1905 *New York* received a major refit. Her six old 8in/35 guns were replaced by four modern 8in/45 guns in new elliptical turrets, while the outdated secondary battery was upgraded to ten 5in/50 RF guns. Machinery was heavily overhauled and much of the hull replaced.

On February 16, 1911, *New York* was renamed *Saratoga*, after the small town in upstate New York. However, on August 29, 1916, Congress authorized the USN's first six battlecruisers, the 35,000-ton Lexington-class; of which the third unit was to be named *Saratoga*, in honor not of the New York town, but the 1777 battle fought nearby. On December 1, 1917, armored cruiser *Saratoga* was again stripped of her name and duly re-christened *Rochester*, after the city in western New York. Simultaneously, *Rochester*'s tertiary battery and after 5in guns were removed and replaced with two 3in AA guns.

New York-class specifications (1893)

Length:	380ft 6in
Beam:	64ft 10in
Draft:	23ft 3in
Displacement:	8,200 tons
Propulsion:	Four three-cylinder VTE engines
Speed:	21 knots at 17,401ihp
Range:	4,800nm radius at 10 knots
Coal capacity:	750 tons normal; 1,279 tons maximum
Armament:	Six 8in/35 BL rifles
	Twelve 4in/40 RF guns
	Eight 6-pdrs, four 1-pdrs, four 0.50-caliber Gatlings
	Three above-water 18in Whitehead torpedo tubes
Protection:	Belt: 4in
	Deck: 3–6in
	Conning tower: 7.5in
	Main turrets: 5.5in, barbettes 10in
Complement:	40 officers, 526 enlisted
Cost:	$2.99 million

New York-class construction

Ship	Built at	Yard	Laid down	Launched	Commissioned	Fate
ACR-2 *New York*	Philadelphia, PA	William Cramp & Sons	Sep 19, 1890	Dec 2, 1891	Aug 1, 1893	Hulk scuttled Dec 24, 1941

USS *Brooklyn* (1896)

On July 19, 1892, Congress authorized one 9,000-ton battleship and one 8,000-ton armored cruiser. These eventually became the "sea-going

SPANISH-AMERICAN WAR 1898

New York and *Brooklyn* are both seen in 1898, when their peacetime white and ocher have been temporarily painted out with a dull wartime haze gray. After the war both cruisers would be painted back into their bright peacetime colors. Only in early 1909 did the USN switch to a permanent haze gray.

1. *New York* (ACR-2) is viewed above in her role as Rear Admiral William T. Sampson's North Atlantic Squadron flagship. A major 1905 refit saw much of the cruiser's hull replaced entirely. *New York* received a brand-new main deck, gun deck, and double-bottom. *New York*'s main turrets with their four 8in/35 guns were replaced by new balanced turrets mounting four modern 8in/45 Mk 6 guns, while *New York*'s amidships 8in/35 guns were permanently removed. Ten carriage-mounted 5in/50 Mk 6 RF guns replaced *New York*'s weak and outdated 4in/40 secondary battery, while *New York*'s bow and stern torpedo tubes were unshipped. *New York*'s machinery received a major overhaul, including the replacement of her obsolete fire-tube boilers with 12 modern Pratt & Whitney boilers. To accommodate the increased power, *New York*'s funnels were raised in height from how they are depicted here. After *New York*'s 1905 refit it was virtually a new warship. Despite being the oldest US armored cruiser, after the modernization *New York* had now become one of the most modern.

2. Below is *Brooklyn* (ACR-3) in her wartime role as Commodore Winfield Scott Schley's Flying Squadron flagship. *Brooklyn*'s bow and stern torpedo tubes were removed in 1899, and both her 8in/35 and 5in/40 RF batteries were overhauled. Much of *Brooklyn*'s flammable material was stripped or covered with asbestos. In 1901, after continued structural problems with *Brooklyn*'s secondary battery, the USN replaced all 12 of her 5in/40 guns and their mounts with new guns of all-steel construction. A 1902 refit overhauled *Brooklyn*'s machinery and enlarged her fore bridge, while in 1904 a wireless system was installed.

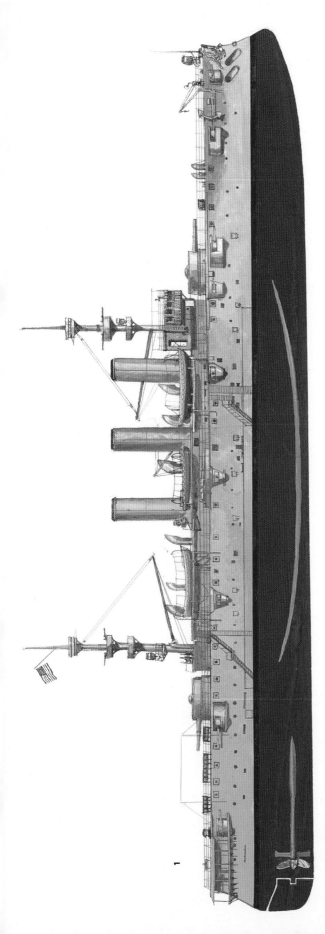

1

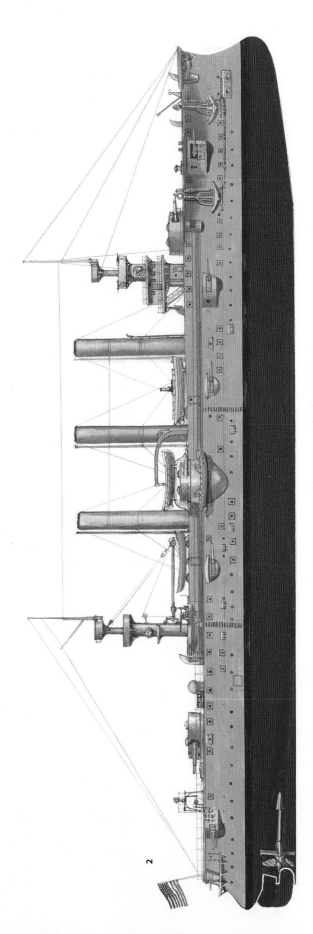

2

A view of USS *Brooklyn*'s bridge and forward 8in turret in late 1898, showing the location that Yeoman George Ellis was killed by a Spanish shell during Santiago. *Brooklyn*'s fighting bridges are also visible, and above them is a fighting top on *Brooklyn*'s foremast. (LC-DIG-det-4a14822)

battleship" *Iowa* (BB-4) and the armored cruiser *Brooklyn* (ACR-3). *Iowa* and *Brooklyn* were designed and contracted simultaneously. USN steel warship design remained in an experimental stage and was still heavily influenced by European concepts. Both *Iowa* and *Brooklyn* employed a severe tumblehome hull, visibly representing the USN's brief infatuation with French naval design. *Brooklyn* was commissioned in December 1896. At a final 9,215 tons, *Brooklyn* was 1,000 tons larger than *New York*, allowing substantial improvements in firepower, range, and seakeeping.

Brooklyn mounted eight 8in/35 guns in four twin turrets in a lozenge arrangement. *Brooklyn*'s new forecastle raised both freeboard and the forward 8in turret 8ft higher than in *New York*. *Brooklyn*'s amidships 8in turrets were mounted in huge, outlying sponsons. This arrangement combined with the severe tumblehome hull to give *Brooklyn*'s wing turrets true fore-and-aft firing arcs. *Brooklyn*'s secondary battery comprised 12 5in/40 RF guns, 12 Driggs-Schroeder 6-pdrs, four 1-pdrs, and four Colt automatic machine guns. *Brooklyn* additionally mounted five 18in Whitehead torpedo tubes.

A 192ft long, 3in thick Harvey belt protected *Brooklyn*'s machinery at the waterline, while up to 8in Harvey armor protected the 8in turrets. Four inches of nickel-steel armored *Brooklyn*'s 5in gun sponsons and shields, while a 3in thick mild steel protective deck stretched *Brooklyn*'s full length.

Brooklyn was built at Philadelphia's Cramp yard. Cramp's original design would have been powered by two advanced new vertical quadruple expansion engines on two shafts, with the fourth expansion cylinder on each engine able to disengage for economical cruising. This scheme offered a smaller and lighter powerplant, more efficient use of steam, and prevented the unequal wear expected when coupling two engines to the same shaft, as on *New York*. The USN ultimately rejected this layout, choosing to install a

Brooklyn viewed from her starboard quarter, c.1897–1901. Her starboard 8in gun turret sponson can be seen amidships, visibly protruding from *Brooklyn*'s sharply inward-sloping tumblehome hull. The USN would not commission another warship with such a pronounced tumblehome until guided missile destroyer USS *Zumwalt* (DDG-1000) in 2016. (LC-DIG-det-4a14042)

copy of *New York*'s VTE arrangement with minor improvements, including taller 100ft funnels for additional induced draft.

Brooklyn-class specifications (1896)

Length:	400ft 6in
Beam:	64ft 8in
Draft:	24ft
Displacement:	9,215 tons
Propulsion:	Four three-cylinder VTE engines
Speed:	21.9 knots at 18,769ihp
Range:	6,088nm radius at 10 knots
Coal capacity:	900 tons normal, 1,461 tons maximum
Armament:	Eight 8in/35 BL rifles
	Twelve 5in/40 RF guns
	Twelve 6-pdrs, four 1-pdrs, four 0.30-caliber MGs
	Four 18in Whitehead torpedo tubes
Protection:	Belt: 3in
	Deck: 3–6in
	Conning tower: 8.5in
	Main turrets: 5.5in, barbettes: 4–8in
Complement:	46 officers, 470 enlisted
Cost:	$3.45 million

Brooklyn-class construction

Ship	Built at	Yard	Laid down	Launched	Commissioned	Fate
ACR-3 *Brooklyn*	Philadelphia, PA	William Cramp & Sons	Aug 2, 1893	Oct 2, 1895	Dec 1, 1896	Sold Dec 20, 1921

The "Big Ten" armored cruisers 1905–08

The 1898 war demonstrated that the USN lacked "large, swift, and powerful armored cruisers of great coal endurance." Additionally, the subsequent Spanish-American War spoils meant the United States suddenly possessed territories and responsibilities stretching into the Caribbean and across the vast Pacific. Accordingly, subsequent USN design doctrine would stress enormous steaming endurance.

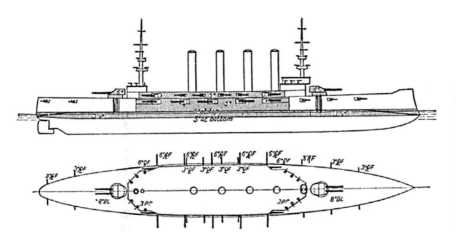

Pennsylvania mounted a 6in thick waterline belt of Krupp armor, plus 5in of side armor amidships. Up to 4in nickel-steel comprised her protective deck. *Pennsylvania*, *West Virginia*, and *California* were originally to have been sheathed in copper below the waterline, but this plan was ultimately dropped. (Author's collection)

By 1899, USN doctrine had fully converted to offensive sea control by concentrated battle fleets. Armored cruisers' new role was to function as a high-speed wing for the US battle fleet, striking ahead of US battleships and sweeping aside the enemy's escorts to force a decisive fleet engagement. Commissioned between 1905 and 1908, this second generation of six Pennsylvania- and four Tennessee-class vessels was collectively known as the "Big Ten" armored cruisers. All were designed as flagships and accordingly mounted two full bridges, one each fore and aft. The Big Ten cruisers were so large and expensive that each essentially removed a potential battleship from USN building plans. Between 1904 and 1912 the USN's desired number of battleships was ultimately authorized and built, but only by sacrificing planned requests to Congress for battlecruisers.

Pennsylvania-class (1905–08)

On March 3, 1899, Congress authorized three new armored cruisers, to displace 12,000 tons and "carrying the heaviest armor and most powerful ordnance for vessels of their class." At least one was to be built on the West Coast. A second, identical authorization followed on June 7, 1900, for a total of six armored cruisers of the same class. The lead ship, ACR-4, was originally to have been named *Nebraska*, but on March 7, 1901, the USN swapped *Nebraska*'s name with the Virginia-class battleship BB-14. The Nebraska-class armored cruiser thus became the Pennsylvania-class.

High speed required heavy machinery and long hulls, which were expensive both in design and cost. The Pennsylvanias displaced 13,680 tons, barely 1,000 tons less than the Virginia-class battleships, but were 63ft longer. At 502ft, the Pennsylvanias were the longest warships the USN had yet built, while their complement of 832 men was 20 more than in the Virginias. All six Pennsylvanias were contracted for between $3.7–3.9 million each, but construction of the West Coast cruisers, *California* and *South Dakota*, proved tortured, partly because most parts had to be built in the eastern United States and shipped west. However, three major labor strikes and the 1906 San Francisco earthquake caused further delays, with *California* requiring five years, seven months to build, and *South Dakota* seven years. Final costs for

C PENNSYLVANIA-CLASS

1. Pennsylvania-class cruiser USS *Colorado* (ACR-7) is viewed upon her commissioning on January 19, 1905. Built at Philadelphia's Cramp yard, *Colorado* was the first "Big Ten" cruiser commissioned. She appears here in the Pennsylvania-class's original configuration. On September 5, 1905, Russia and Japan would sign the September 5, 1905 Treaty of Portsmouth that would end the Russo-Japanese War and ultimately deliver President Theodore Roosevelt a Nobel Peace Prize. *Colorado* was one of the vessels that escorted Roosevelt back to Washington, DC on his triumphant return from New Hampshire.

2. At bottom, class lead ship USS *Pennsylvania* (ACR-4) is depicted on January 18, 1911, while moored in San Francisco Bay for Eugene Ely's historic landing attempt. *Pennsylvania*'s temporary landing deck had been constructed a few weeks earlier. Mounted over the stern, it was 130ft long and 32ft wide and constructed of pine planks. The platform's aftermost 10ft hung over *Pennsylvania*'s stern at a 30-degree angle, dropping 4ft. The remaining 120ft was inclined slightly uphill to help slow Ely's plane as he landed.

To help arrest Ely's plane, a series of 21 transverse ropes, with 50lb sandbags at each end, were suspended eight inches above the landing platform by boards laid the length of the deck. Canvas awnings were rigged both in front and to the sides of *Pennsylvania*'s landing platform to help snag Ely's plane in the event of an errant landing. The arresting wire system worked so well that it is still the standard system used today.

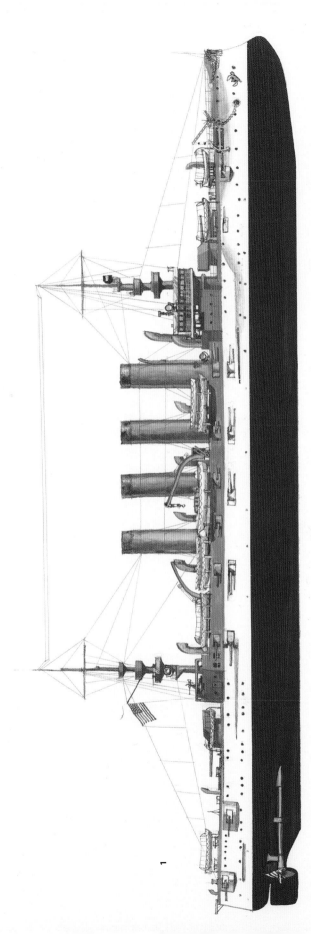

1

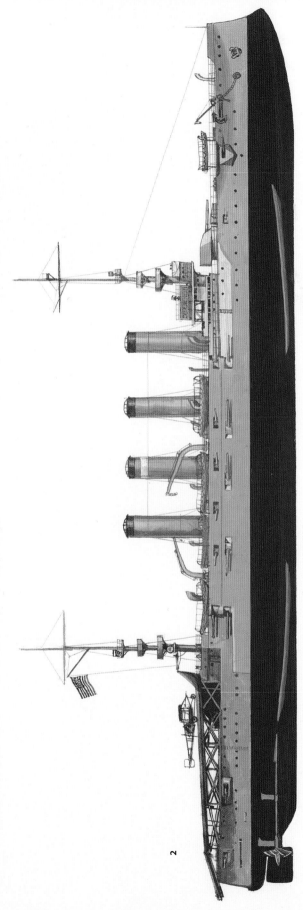

2

Pennsylvania shows off the temporary landing platform built over her stern at San Francisco's Hunter's Point, January 1911. Despite frigid conditions, Ely would land successfully on *Pennsylvania's* stern on January 18, 1911. He was congratulated by his waiting wife, and given a celebratory lunch by the ship's officers below decks, before taking off again an hour later. (NH 70595)

the Pennsylvanias were between $5.6 million and $5.7 million each.

Pennsylvania mounted four 8in/40 guns in two balanced, elliptical, sloped face Mk12 turrets. By 1900 the American ordnance industry fully equaled Europe's, allowing *Pennsylvania* a proper secondary battery of 14 6in/50 RF guns. Additional batteries were 16 3in/50 RF guns, two 6-pdrs, and eight 1-pdrs. *Pennsylvania* carried eight torpedoes for her two submerged 18in torpedo tubes, the result of 1903 Naval War College games.

A 244ft long, 6in thick Krupp belt protected *Pennsylvania's* waterline, with 5in of Krupp side armor extending upwards from the belt to the main deck and shielding the 6in battery. Two transverse bulkheads of 4in Harvey steel completed *Pennsylvania's* armored citadel. The 8in turrets received 6.5in Krupp armor and the conning tower 9in. Between 1.5in and 4in nickel-steel comprised *Pennsylvania's* full-length armored deck.

Two four-cylinder VTEs delivered a combined 23,000ihp to two shafts. Cramp installed *Pennsylvania* and *Colorado* with 32 Niclausse boilers each. The remaining four cruisers' steam was provided by 16 Babcock & Wilcox water-tube boilers. Sixteen blowers provided each cruiser's forced draft, with four 100ft funnels expelling exhaust. Nominal coal bunkerage was 900 tons normal and 2,000 tons full. *Pennsylvania's* powerplants were the most powerful installed on a US warship until the dreadnought battleships *Delaware* (BB-28) and *North Dakota* (BB-29) were commissioned in 1910.

Pennsylvania-class specifications (1905)

Length:	502ft
Beam:	69ft 6in
Draft:	24ft 1in
Displacement:	13,680 tons
Propulsion:	Two four-cylinder VTE engines
Speed:	22.4 knots at 28,600ihp
Range:	6,840nm radius at 10 knots (South Dakota)
Coal capacity:	900 tons normal, 2,025 tons maximum
Armament:	Four 8in/40 BL rifles
	Fourteen 6in/50 RF guns
	Sixteen 3in/50 RF guns
	Two 6-pdrs, eight 1-pdrs
	Two 18in Whitehead torpedo tubes
Protection:	Belt: 6in Krupp, side 5in Krupp
	Deck: 1.5–6in nickel-steel
	Conning tower: 9in Krupp
	Main turrets: 6.5in Krupp, barbettes 6in Krupp
Complement:	41 officers, 791 enlisted
Cost:	$5.7 million

Pennsylvania-class construction

Ship	Built at	Yard	Laid down	Launched	Commissioned	Fate
ACR-4 *Pennsylvania*	Philadelphia, PA	William Cramp & Sons	Aug 7, 1901	Aug 22, 1903	Mar 9, 1905	Struck Oct 26, 1931
ACR-5 *West Virginia*	Newport News, VA	Newport News Shipbuilding	Sep 16, 1901	Apr 18, 1903	Feb 23, 1905	Struck Mar 12, 1930
ACR-6 *California*	San Francisco, CA	Union Iron Works	May 7, 1902	Apr 28, 1904	Aug 1, 1907	Sunk by German mine Jul 19, 1918
ACR-7 *Colorado*	Philadelphia, PA	William Cramp & Sons	Apr 25, 1901	Apr 25, 1903	Jan 19, 1905	Struck Feb 21, 1930
ACR-8 *Maryland*	Newport News, VA	Newport News Shipbuilding	Oct 7, 1901	Sep 12, 1903	Apr 18, 1905	Struck Nov 13, 1929
ACR-9 *South Dakota*	San Francisco, CA	Union Iron Works	Sep 30, 1902	Jul 21, 1904	Jan 27, 1908	Struck Nov 15, 1929

Tennessee-class (1906–08)

On July 1, 1902, Congress authorized "two first-class armored cruisers of not more than 14,500 tons … carrying the heaviest armor and most powerful armament for vessels of their class and [having] the highest practical speed and great radius of action …" The resulting Tennessee-class armored cruisers were designed as improved Pennsylvanias and built to a modified *Pennsylvania* hull design. The Tennessees' machinery essentially duplicated that of the last two Pennsylvanias, the *California* and *South Dakota*. At 502ft long, a slightly widened 73ft beam gave the Tennessees a 6.9-to-1 hull ratio compared to the Pennsylvanias' 7.2-to-1. However, the Tennessees' hull was finer below the waterline, allowing 22 knots.

Within the Board on Construction the Tennessees were quietly referred to as "fast battleships," a designation that would no doubt have outraged Congress. Indeed, *Tennessee* outgunned virtually every existing armored cruiser in the world; its total weight of broadside was 47.5 percent greater than *Pennsylvania*'s, inspiring the term "cruiser destroyer." The class's four 10in/40 and 16 6in/50 RF guns comprised the heaviest US cruiser battery ever mounted until the 1944 Alaska-class.

Armored cruiser USS *Washington* at Puget Sound, 1908. She is framed against the snowy 7,980ft Olympic Mountains in its eponymous state. Opposite *Washington* and out of view behind the photographer is the city of Seattle and the ice-capped 14,410ft Mount Rainier volcano. (NH 63652)

A post-modernization *Montana* is seen underway *c.*1914. The Tennessee-class essentially duplicated the machinery of the Pennsylvania-class cruisers *California* and *South Dakota*. All US armored cruisers were powered by traditional Vertical Triple Expansion (VTE) steam engines, rather than the revolutionary new marine turbine. (LC-DIG-det-4a16280)

Tennessee's 10in battery was mounted in twin turrets a lofty 30ft above the waterline, while four of *Tennessee*'s 16 6in guns were sited 25ft above the waterline in main deck sponsons and capable of fore or aft fire. The remaining 12 6in guns were mounted in embrasures along the broadside, although the four corner guns could each fire directly forward or aft. With their high placement and clear firing arcs, *Tennessee*'s gun arrangement far exceeded that mounted by contemporary British armored cruisers. After fierce debate, the Tennessee-class ultimately received four submerged 21in Bliss-Leavitt torpedo tubes.

The Tennessees devoted 2,555 tons to protection, a 14 percent increase over the Pennsylvanias on essentially the same hull. The Board's Chief Constructor F. T. Bowles, Admiral Bradford, and Captain Sigsbee had all urged protection over speed, with Sigsbee arguing, "The aim is to get these cruisers in the battle line …" Congress authorized an additional two Tennessees on April 27, 1904, incorporating some minor improvements. Armor thicknesses were slightly rearranged, the old and ineffective cellulose cofferdams were discarded, and internal stowage was adjusted to afford 20 percent more 10in and 6in ammunition as well as 200 tons additional coal.

The original 1902 authorizations, *Tennessee* and *Washington*, were commissioned in 1906. The improved 1904 cruisers, *North Carolina* and *Montana*, followed in 1908. The well-balanced Tennessees proved several

D TENNESSEE AND ST. LOUIS CLASSES

1. Tennessee-class armored cruiser USS *Tennessee* (ACR-10) is viewed above in her original configuration shortly after her July 17, 1906 commissioning. She still retains the standard pole masts from its original design, as she would not receive a cage foremast until mid-1911. As improved Pennsylvanias, the Tennessees cut very similar lines. *Tennessee*'s 10in turrets however are noticeably larger than the 8in turrets aboard *Pennsylvania*. Additionally, *Pennsylvania*'s 8in barbettes were not heavily armored throughout their full length, an issue corrected on the Tennessee-class's 10in barbettes. Because *Tennessee* had a finer hull below the waterline, most of the Tennessee-class's additional displacement over the Pennsylvania-class was dedicated to increased firepower and protection, rather than machinery. The Tennessees additionally proved to be good seakeepers, being fairly stable and mostly pitching rather than rolling.

2. At bottom is St. Louis-class semi-armored cruiser USS *St. Louis* (C-22), depicted in June 1917 while she escorted the first American Expeditionary Force convoy to France. *St. Louis* had been in reserve commission at Honolulu since July 1916, where she served as a Pacific Fleet submarine tender and as a Pearl Harbor station ship. On February 4, 1917, a *St. Louis* boarding party successfully stormed the interned German cruiser SMS *Geier* when it became clear *Geier*'s crew was attempting to scuttle her. Once the United States declared war on April 6, 1917, *St. Louis* steamed for San Diego, where she was returned to full commission on April 20.

St. Louis then reinforced the Atlantic Fleet, transporting six companies of marines from Panama to Cuba in May. By June 1917 she had been transferred to the newly established Cruiser and Transport Force that would transport and escort AEF convoys to Europe. Within months *St. Louis* would lose two 6in/50 guns and 14 3in/50 guns, all of which went to arm US merchantmen. In their place *St. Louis* received two 3in/50 anti-aircraft guns. After the armistice, *St. Louis* would complete seven round-trip voyages repatriating 8,437 doughboys back to the United States.

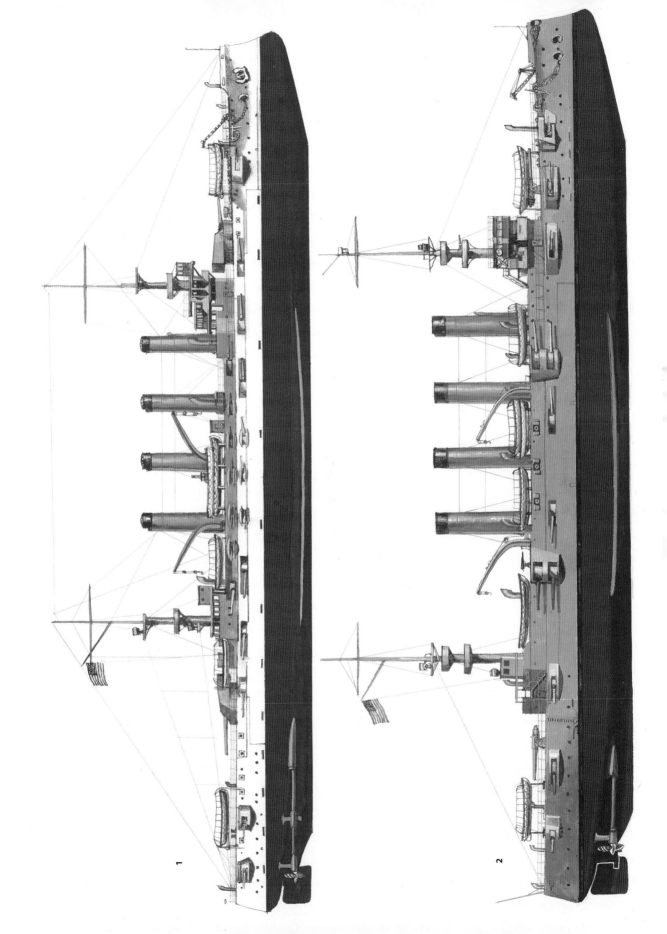

knots faster than the IJN's 12in-gunned, 20-knot Tsukaba- and Kurama-class proto-battlecruisers, while being themselves more heavily armed than any other armored cruiser. Although shortly rendered obsolete by the Invincible-class battlecruisers, the Tennessees' combination of speed and firepower made them arguably the finest armored cruisers ever built.

Tennessee-class specifications (1906)	
Length:	502ft
Beam:	72ft 11in
Draft:	25ft
Displacement:	14,500 tons
Propulsion:	Two four-cylinder VTEs
Speed:	22.1 knots at 26,963ihp
Range:	5,423nm radius at 10 knots
Coal capacity:	900 tons normal, 2,020 tons maximum
Armament:	Four 10in/40 BL rifles
	Sixteen 6in/50 RF guns
	Twenty-two 3in/50 RF guns
	Two 1-pdrs, eight .30-caliber machine guns
	Four submerged 21in Bliss-Leavitt torpedo tubes
Protection:	Belt: 6in Krupp, side 5in Krupp
	Deck: 1.5–4in nickel-steel
	Conning tower: 9in Krupp
	Main turrets: 9in Krupp, barbettes 7in Krupp
Complement:	40 officers, 874 enlisted
Cost:	$6.2 million

Tennessee-class construction						
Ship	Built at	Yard	Laid down	Launched	Commissioned	Fate
ACR-10 Tennessee	Philadelphia, PA	William Cramp & Sons	Jun 20, 1903	Dec 3, 1904	Jul 17, 1906	Destroyed by freak wave Aug 29, 1916
ACR-11 Washington	Camden, NJ	New York Shipbuilding	Sep 23, 1903	Mar 18, 1905	Aug 7, 1906	Struck Jul 19, 1946
ACR-12 North Carolina	Newport News, VA	Newport News Shipbuilding	Mar 1, 1905	Oct 6, 1906	May 7, 1908	Struck Jul 15, 1930
ACR-13 Montana	Newport News, VA	Newport News Shipbuilding	Apr 29, 1905	Dec 15, 1906	Jul 21, 1908	Struck Jul 15, 1930

Semi-armored cruisers 1905–06

St. Louis-class (1905–06)

After crushing Spain, the United States suddenly found itself a global power. Accordingly, in November 1898 Navy Secretary John D. Long requested an additional three battleships, three 12,000-ton armored cruisers (the future Pennsylvania-class), six 2,500-ton "peace" cruisers, and three 6,000-ton protected cruisers of an improved *Olympia* type. Congress approved all but the Olympias, but this preserved the *Olympia* design for further tinkering.

By 1899 the USN conceived the improved Olympias as 20-knot protected cruisers mounting two 8in guns and a secondary battery of ten

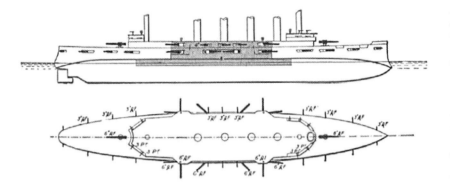

6in or 14 5in guns. However, under construction in Philadelphia's Cramp yard was the 23-knot, 6,700-ton Russian cruiser *Varyag*. Concerned at the 3-knot disadvantage, in November 1899 Long again requested his three improved Olympias, but this time at 8,000 tons for increased performance.

Congress now approved Long's request, and on June 7, 1900 authorized three 8,000-ton protected cruisers. However, by July 2 the Board on Construction had decided to fit the new class with certain armored cruiser features, including twin screws, more robust auxiliary machinery, and enlarged coal spaces, which increased the design to 8,500 tons. The Board then added a partial, armored cruiser-style 4in waterline belt protecting the machinery spaces only, with a centrally located zone of 4in thick side armor extending fully to the top of the ship. However, the additional weight required a dangerous thinning of deck armor. Restoring a sloped 3in protective deck further increased displacement. Armament was set at 14 6in/50 RF guns, 18 3in/50 RF guns, 12 3-pdrs, eight 1-pdrs, and four .30-caliber automatic guns. No torpedo tubes were mounted.

According to naval historian Norman Friedman, "These ships were among the earliest well-documented examples of creeping growth in warship design." At a calculated (and stripped down) 9,592 tons trials displacement, the design was 20 percent over the congressional authorization, causing Chief Constructor Philip Hichborn to insist the ship was illegal. In fact, numerous physical, logistic, and legal shortcuts were required even at this displacement. Additionally, by August 1900 a minority Board report claimed the class would be overpowered by the smaller, older *Brooklyn*, and would be outrun by wartime auxiliary cruisers (converted passenger liners). However, the majority report believed modern cruisers demanded side protection at any cost, and ultimately approved the 9,592-ton scheme, which became the St. Louis-class.

U.S. NAVY OFFICIAL PHOTOGRAPH

E

USS *MONTANA* (ACR-13)

Commissioned on July 21, 1908, Tennessee-class armored cruiser USS *Montana* (ACR-13) was the last US armored cruiser ever built, and the last new US cruiser of any kind until 1923. *Montana* is seen here in late 1914, having been heavily modified from her original appearance. By 1909 an overall haze gray paint scheme had replaced *Montana*'s original white and ocher livery and most of her extraneous ornamentation was removed. In July 1914, *Montana* entered Portsmouth for a major overhaul, where she was fitted with a lattice foremast.

KEY

1. 3in/50 RF gun
2. After 10in/40 turret
3. Searchlight
4. Mainmast fighting top
5. Mainmast
6. Funnel
7. Crow's nest
8. Lattice foremast
9. Flying bridge
10. Armored conning tower
11. Forward 10in/40 turret
12. Anchor
13. Hawsepipe
14. 6in/50 RF gun
15. Ship's boat
16. Boiler
17. Four-cylinder Vertical Triple Expansion engine
18. Connecting rod
19. 10in/40 shell hoist
20. Screw
21. Rudder

The USN officially classified the St. Louis-class as "protected cruisers" to legally conform to the original congressional authorization. Indeed, the class's 6in/50 main battery, 4in belt, and 22-knot speed were all depressingly modest on a displacement of nearly 10,000 tons.

St. Louis-class specifications

Length:	424ft
Beam:	66ft
Draft:	22ft 6in
Displacement:	9,700 tons
Propulsion:	Two VTEs on two shafts
Speed:	22.1 knots at 27,264ihp
Coal capacity:	650 tons normal; 1,500 tons max
Armament:	Fourteen 6in/50 RF guns
	Eighteen 3in/50 RF guns
	Twelve 3-pdrs, eight 1-pdrs
	Four .30-caliber machine guns
Protection:	(All armor Harvey-type)
	Belt: 4in
	Deck: 2–3in
	Upper/casemates: 4in
	Conning tower: 5in
Complement:	36 officers, 627 enlisted
Cost:	$2.83 million

St. Louis-class construction

Ship	Built at	Yard	Laid down	Launched	Commissioned	Fate
C-20 St. Louis	Philadelphia, PA	Neafie & Levy	Jul 21, 1902	May 6, 1905	Aug 18, 1906	Struck Mar 20, 1930
C-21 Milwaukee	San Francisco, CA	Union Iron Works	Jul 30, 1902	Sep 10, 1904	Dec 10, 1906	Fatally run aground Jan 13, 1917
C-22 Charleston	Newport News, VA	Newport News Shipbuilding	Jan 30, 1902	Jan 23, 1904	Oct 17, 1905	Struck Nov 25, 1929

OPERATIONAL HISTORY

The Spanish-American War 1898

On February 15, 1898, the USN's original armored cruiser, second-class battleship *Maine*, abruptly exploded while visiting the Spanish colony of Cuba. Spanish-American relations had already been tense, and by late April both countries mutually declared war. *New York* and *Brooklyn* comprised the only armored cruisers in the US fleet, but they were both modern vessels and stationed on the US East Coast.

The USN's war plan was to form a single battle fleet concentrated around its North Atlantic Squadron at Key West, Florida, to operate against Spanish-occupied Cuba and Puerto Rico. However, weeks earlier, on March 24, the commander of the North Atlantic Squadron had suffered a nervous breakdown. The squadron's next senior officer, Captain William T. Sampson, had assumed command on March 27, naming Captain French E. Chadwick's *New York* as his flagship.

Meanwhile, public hysteria had forced the USN to divide its fleet and establish a second, unplanned formation. Based at Hampton Roads, Virginia, this improvised "Flying Squadron" would ostensibly defend the US East Coast. Its commander, Commodore William Scott Schley, would ride Captain Francis Cook's armored cruiser *Brooklyn* as his flagship.

Temporarily promoted to rear admiral, on April 27 Sampson led *New York*, monitor *Puritan*, and protected cruiser *Cincinnati* out of Key West to bombard the Matanzas fortifications near Havana. The following day – obsessed with salvaging national face – the Spanish government dispatched Contraalmirante Pascual Cervera's badly outclassed cruiser squadron across the Atlantic on a clear suicide mission. Under Cervera were the 6,890-ton armored cruisers *Infanta Maria Teresa*, *Vizcaya*, and *Almirante Oquendo*, the 6,840-ton armored cruiser *Cristóbal Colón*, and the 380-ton destroyers *Plutón* and *Furor*. Although impressive on paper, Cervera's ships were horribly dilapidated, manned by poorly trained crews, and in no condition to fight anyone.

Sampson assumed Cervera's destination was San Juan, Puerto Rico. At dawn, May 12, Sampson's North Atlantic Squadron arrived at San Juan with flagship *New York*, battleships *Iowa* and *Indiana*, monitors *Amphitrite* and *Terror*, and torpedo boat *Porter*. With Cervera nowhere to be found, Sampson ordered a general bombardment of San Juan at 0516hrs, opening fire at 1,200yds. When Spanish artillery retaliated, a 5.9in shell struck *New York*, killing one of *New York*'s portside 8in gun crew. After two and a half hours, Sampson ceased fire and returned to Florida, the Americans having lost two killed and three wounded. Total Spanish casualties were seven killed and 52 wounded (including civilians).

The following day, the Navy Department ordered Schley's Flying Squadron to Key West to be put under Sampson's overall command – an awkward arrangement, because as a commodore Schley technically outranked Sampson, whose wartime rank of rear admiral was only temporary. Sampson shortly ordered Schley to southeastern Cuba to search for Cervera. Schley finally discovered Cervera at Santiago, Cuba on May 29, sent a message to Sampson, and ordered a half-hearted blockade. Sampson's *New York* and battleship *Oregon* arrived off Santiago on June 1. Sampson then ordered a tight blockade of the harbor, effectively trapping Cervera's squadron.

The combined US fleet first bombarded Santiago on June 6, temporarily silencing Santiago's Spanish batteries but not destroying them. The Americans shelled Santiago again on June 16, with the same effect. Meanwhile, to envelop Santiago from landwards, Major-General William Shafter's 16,300-strong US V Corps began landing at nearby Daquiri and Siboney on June 22. Over the next week Sampson supported V Corps' ground operations with intermittent bombardments. Then, on July 1, at the Battle of San Juan Hill, Shafter's V Corps won the heights above Santiago harbor, dooming Cervera's squadron. In response, Cuba's governor ordered Cervera to break out of Santiago on a pointless suicide mission.

At 0900hrs, July 3, *New York* signaled to disregard her movements, and steamed east so that Sampson could parlay with Shafter at Siboney, nine miles away. Tactical command of the fleet off Santiago's harbor implicitly fell to Schley in *Brooklyn*. Accompanying *Brooklyn* were battleships *Texas*, *Iowa*, *Oregon*, and *Indiana*, plus gunboats *Vixen* and *Gloucester*.

A respected naval engineer, Rear Admiral William T. Sampson had been named chair of the USN's February 1898 court of inquiry into the *Maine* disaster. A cool and logical man, Sampson was the architect of the highly successful Santiago blockade, but his chilly personality did him little favor with the American news media. (Public Domain)

Unlike the methodical Sampson, Commodore Winfield Scott Schley was a classic sea dog, aggressive and impulsive. However, his odd *Brooklyn* maneuver early in the Santiago battle allowed an opening for the criticism that followed the engagement. During the unfortunate controversy, Schley consistently displayed great magnanimity, refusing to discredit his superior Sampson. (NH 85942)

At 0935hrs the American lookouts sighted Spanish ships steaming for the harbor mouth. Schley snapped, "Go right for them!" A shot fired east alerted Sampson. With *New York* six miles away, Sampson immediately turned *New York* about and ordered maximum speed. As Schley's and Cervera's ships charged each other off Santiago, a huge confusing mêlée broke out, with American and Spanish guns producing a virtually impenetrable smokescreen hanging on the water. Meanwhile, ordered by Cervera, *Infanta Maria Teresa* charged *Brooklyn* in an apparently sacrificial attempt to ram Schley's flagship. Upon seeing *Infanta Maria Teresa* on course to ram *Brooklyn* head-on, Schley ordered a hard turn to starboard (northeast), away from the Spanish ships and into the course of the pursuing US battleships. When warned *Brooklyn* was crossing into battleship *Texas'* path, Schley allegedly responded, "Damn the *Texas*, let her look out for herself!" According to *Texas'* Captain John Philip, *Brooklyn* suddenly loomed out of the smoke "as big as half a dozen *Great Easterns*, and … so near that it took our breath away." Philip ordered all engines full reverse, destroying *Texas'* pursuit momentum and nearly bringing the battleship to a complete stop.

Highly accurate in its details, this 1899 painting portrays the initial Santiago mêlée. The Spanish cruisers can be seen exiting the harbor in single file, with Cervera's flagship *Infanta Maria Theresa* attempting to ram Schley's flagship *Brooklyn*. Behind *Brooklyn* is battleship *Texas*, which will nearly collide with *Brooklyn* itself in the subsequent confusion. (Public Domain)

Brooklyn's seemingly flippant maneuver had nearly caused a catastrophic collision. Apparently oblivious, *Brooklyn* continued through a full clockwise loop until once again headed back towards the battle. Meanwhile, in the confused free-for-all, all four Spanish cruisers broke away to the west, leaving the US ships to pursue them along the Cuban coast, pounding them mercilessly. By 1015hrs *Infanta Maria Teresa* was burning uncontrollably. Cervera struck his colors and ordered her aground. It was followed minutes later by the blazing *Almirante Oquendo*.

Brooklyn and battleship *Oregon*, the two fastest ships in Schley's squadron, were soon leading the pursuit. Struggling to reach the battle, by 1000hrs *New York* had returned within range of Santiago's harbor forts, which opened fire.

Destroyed Spanish cruisers *Almirante Oquendo* and *Infanta Maria Theresa* are seen run aground and burning off the coast of southeastern Cuba shortly after the Battle of Santiago, June 3, 1898. Although American gunnery was generally poor, the 8in/35 guns performed best. Fortunately for the Americans, Spanish gunnery was abysmal. (NH 2681)

Focused on the fleeing Spanish cruisers, Sampson refused Captain Chadwick's pleas to retaliate. As *New York* crossed the harbor mouth, it observed gunboat *Gloucester* aggressively attacking Spanish destroyers *Plutón* and *Furor* as they emerged from the harbor. *New York's* bow 4in guns fired three shots at Spanish destroyer *Furor*, *New York's* only shots of the battle. *Gloucester* shortly sank *Plutón*, before running *Furor* aground. From *New York's* forecastle, Chadwick waved his cap and led "wild cheers for the plucky little *Gloucester*."

Charging hard west, *New York* was now making 16 knots, her maximum on two engines. Chadwick recalled *New York* "was quivering fore and aft, and had set up the pleasant jingling of metallic objects on the bridge which we knew meant high speed." To save coal and maintenance, both *Brooklyn* and *New York* had left their forward engines uncoupled throughout the blockade. Bringing all four engines online required coming to a complete stop to recouple, a time-killing process which neither Sampson nor Schley was inclined to do.

Brooklyn also topped out at 16 knots on her two engaged engines. Worried the fleeing *Vizcaya* and *Cristóbal Colón* were pulling away from *Brooklyn*, Schley ordered Chief Yeoman George H. Ellis, exposed on *Brooklyn*'s forecastle, to continue taking readings. Ellis, an expert with the stadimeter, reported that the Spanish cruisers were maintaining range, but Schley disagreed: "No, they are evidently gaining." As Ellis strode to the forward 8in turret to verify his earlier reading, a Spanish shell struck him in the face and decapitated him. Schley had been standing ten feet behind Ellis and the headless corpse erupted blood over Schley and several others. Two *Brooklyn* sailors picked up Ellis' body and carried it to the side. "No," Schley shouted, "don't throw that body overboard." Moved at Ellis' bravery and sacrifice, Schley was determined Ellis receive a proper Christian burial. Ellis' body was laid behind the forward 8in turret and covered with a blanket. He would later be buried above Guantánamo.

Minutes later, an 8in shell from *Brooklyn* or possibly *Oregon* struck *Vizcaya* just after 1100hrs and ignited her torpedo tubes. *Vizcaya* exploded, the bow disintegrating and sending fire raging throughout the ship. Striking her colors, the dying *Vizcaya* turned into the coast at 1106hrs.

Now only *Cristóbal Colón* was left, hugging the shore several miles ahead of the lead American pursuers *Brooklyn* and *Oregon*. Much further back charged *New York*. Over the next two hours the Americans slowly gained on the faltering *Cristóbal Colón*. Inevitably the Cuban coast jutted seawards, trapping *Cristóbal Colón* against *Brooklyn*, *Oregon*, and the trailing *New York*. With *Oregon*'s 13in guns now scoring near-misses, *Cristóbal Colón* hauled down her ensign at 1315hrs and ran herself aground.

Fifteen minutes later *Brooklyn* pulled alongside *Cristóbal Colón*. *Brooklyn*'s Captain Cook led a single boat to *Cristóbal Colón* to receive the Spanish vessel's surrender. *Cristóbal Colón*'s Capitán Moreau received Cook, announcing tearfully, "I surrender. You are too much for us." Cervera's second-in-command, Commodore Paredes, "was much overcome by grief, and sobbed bitterly." After brief pleasantries, Cook politely informed the Spaniards their surrender must be unconditional.

New York pulled up at 1443hrs, just as Cook was departing *Cristóbal Colón*. From *Brooklyn*, a giddy Schley signaled, "The enemy has surrendered." After receiving no response for "quite half an hour," Schley hoisted a second signal: "We have gained a great victory." Sampson brusquely responded, "Report your casualties." *Brooklyn* had suffered just one wounded and the

Spanish cruiser *Vizcaya* explodes off the coast of Cuba in the afternoon of July 3, 1898. It had been earlier run aground and abandoned. As *Vizcaya*'s surviving crew and captain were being pulled aboard by battleship *Iowa*, its still blazing fires eventually detonated its magazines. (LC-DIG-det-4a15180)

US fleet's sole fatality, Yeoman Ellis. Schley's *Brooklyn* had suffered 20 hits but little real damage, while Sampson's *New York* remained awkwardly unscathed.

On July 10–11 Sampson's fleet again bombarded Santiago, which finally surrendered on July 17. The Spanish government accepted US terms on August 7. Two weeks later, Sampson's *New York* and Schley's *Brooklyn* led

SCHLEY'S FLAGSHIP USS *BROOKLYN* DUELS SPANISH CRUISER *VIZCAYA* AT THE BATTLE OF SANTIAGO DE CUBA, JULY 3, 1898

Spanish cruiser *Vizcaya* had been commissioned in 1893. She mounted two 11in guns, ten 5.5in guns, eight 6-pdrs, and ten machine guns, plus eight torpedo tubes. *Vizcaya* had actually visited New York in February 1898, where her captain allegedly "hinted at his ability to blow holes in New York skyscrapers." Like the rest of Cervera's ships, *Vizcaya* was forced to go to war in wretched condition. She was long overdue for drydocking and her badly fouled bottom crippled her theoretical top speed of 20 knots. *Vizcaya*'s guns and ammunition were also largely defective. *Vizcaya*'s Capitán Don Antonio Eulate later reported to Cervera, "The deficiencies of these guns were numerous, chief among them, as you already know, the fact that the breech could not be closed, the projectiles jammed, and the firing pins failed to act …. In spite of these defects, the enthusiasm and intelligence of the officers and the excellent discipline of their crews made it possible to fire 150 rounds with the port battery." Additionally, the Spanish crews were poorly trained and did not lay their guns well.

By 1030hrs the lead US ship, Schley's flagship *Brooklyn*, had closed *Vizcaya* and the two cruisers engaged in a running gunnery duel. As *Brooklyn* pursued *Vizcaya*, Commodore Schley told *Brooklyn*'s Captain Cook, "Keep the boys below informed of all the movements. They can't see; and they want to know." Constant messages were sent to *Brooklyn*'s men below, inspiring frequent cheers that reverberated up the ventilators and could be heard on deck. During the firefight, Schley believed *Brooklyn* never exceeded 2,400yds from *Vizcaya* and late in the battle *Brooklyn* closed to 950yds. *Vizcaya* scored several hits on *Brooklyn* with her 5.5in guns, but received numerous 8in, 5in, and 6-pdr hits from *Brooklyn* in return.

Vizcaya was heavily armored, with 10in compound steel over her belt and heavy barbettes, but *Brooklyn*'s better-trained gunners soon told on *Vizcaya*'s less-protected secondary batteries. After casualties, malfunction, and battle damage had virtually silenced *Vizcaya*'s port guns, Eulate resolved to ram *Brooklyn*. Viewed from *Brooklyn*, at 1100hrs *Vizcaya* unexpectedly swung to port, seemingly to turn towards her attackers, when almost instantaneously *Vizcaya*'s bow exploded violently near the waterline – probably a *Brooklyn* 8in shell hit on a bow torpedo tube. Eulate, badly wounded, turned over command of *Vizcaya* to his executive officer and ordered him not to surrender but to beach or scuttle the ship.

Moments later, with smoke pouring from all hatches, *Vizcaya* turned to starboard and headed for shore, listing so badly to port that Schley thought she was going to capsize. *Brooklyn*'s men then clearly observed another American shell rake through *Vizcaya*'s entire length. *Vizcaya* was blazing heavily at the stern; as the Spanish cruisers had many wood furnishings the crew hadn't stripped for battle as the Americans had done. Schley was now convinced that *Vizcaya* was going to sink in deep water before she could reach the safety of shore.

Behind *Brooklyn*, Captain John Philip of battleship *Texas* could see *Vizcaya*'s flames blazing as high as the cruiser's funnel tops, and could see and hear burning, shrieking men throwing themselves into the sea. *Texas*' men cheered, but Philip immediately admonished them, "Don't cheer, boys! Those poor fellows are dying!"

New York's Captain Chadwick recalled that *Vizcaya* "turned in with colors down, and headed for the beach. She steamed in rather slowly, and at such short distance crossed our bows, that the crews were virtually face-to-face, and we looked at each other – victors and vanquished – the former without a cheer, the latter huddled forward, clear of the flames, without sound or movement." As *New York* surged past the burning, exploding *Vizcaya*, several of *New York*'s men noticed a terrified Spaniard struggling in the water, screaming, "¡Madre de Dios, ayúdame!" ("Mother of God, help me!") The battle had interrupted *New York*'s Sunday morning service, conveniently leaving the chaplain's pulpit for the Americans to throw overboard in a desperate attempt to help. "Cling to the cross!" advised an American coxswain. No one, however, saw whether the Spaniard reached it.

Once *Vizcaya* had struck its colors and turned in for the beach, Schley could see that the remaining Spanish cruiser *Cristóbal Colón* was out of range for the moment. Schley therefore ordered *Brooklyn* to cease firing and had Cook order the men out of the hot turrets to rest for a while and enjoy the cool air.

New York pulls up alongside *Brooklyn* at the close of the Santiago battle. Although engaged in numerous bombardments of Cuba and Puerto Rico, horrible luck doomed *New York* to be just out of range for most of the Santiago action. Although fired upon by coast forts and Cervera's cruisers, she suffered the indignity of not being hit once. (Author's collection)

Commodore Winfield Scott Schley photographed on the deck of *Brooklyn*, sometime during the Spanish-American War. Schley's heavy coat suggests this photograph was taken during the spring of 1898. Before his appointment as Flying Squadron commander, Schley had previously been captain of armored cruiser *New York*. (NHHC)

most of the fleet into New York for a triumphant review. Unfortunately, a sordid controversy was already brewing between the two admirals. The commanders' clear personality clash, a ravenous yellow press, and the unlikely and awkward circumstances of July 3, 1898, had produced an unfortunate confluence of events that made controversy inevitable.

Shortly after the July 3 battle, Sampson's staff had telegrammed Secretary of the Navy John D. Long: "The Fleet under my command offers the nation as a Fourth of July present, the whole of Cervera's Fleet." The phrasing echoed Sherman's famous 1864 telegram to Lincoln but failed to mention Schley at all. American journalists embedded within the fleet were outraged by Sampson's apparent slight to Schley, and in their newspaper articles they retaliated by crediting Schley alone with the victory. However, to USN officers, Sampson had planned and executed the successful blockade, while to many officers, *Brooklyn*'s bizarre circle early in the battle appeared to mark Schley as incompetent or even cowardly.

According to a contemporary article, the controversy "arose largely from the determination of the slapdash writers to get a brilliant hero out of the Santiago battle at any cost. Sampson's careful, thorough, and comprehensive leadership would not do at all. The hero must be a dashing and devil-may-care officer, standing on the bridge, and fearlessly leading the line of battle against the enemy fleet."

Both admirals became aware of the growing controversy waged largely by partisan supporters and both attempted to quell it, particularly the aggressively magnanimous Schley. Schley retired in 1901, but that same year a semi-official book, *History of the United States Navy* (approved by Sampson and several USN officers) accused Schley of being a "caitiff, poltroon, and coward." Although President Theodore Roosevelt fired the author, Schley requested a USN court of inquiry to clear his reputation. The court's findings largely went against Schley, although it cleared him of cowardice. The exposure nevertheless increased Schley's public reputation as a war hero. Sampson died the following year, with Schley still protesting the court's decision. Schley would die in 1911, the controversy permanently unresolved.

Atlantic 1899–1917

New York and *Brooklyn* served with the North Atlantic Squadron until the outbreak of the Filipino-American War. *Brooklyn* was detached to the Philippines in late 1899, followed by *New York* in early 1900. For two years the Atlantic was without US armored cruisers, until *Brooklyn* returned to the North Atlantic Squadron in March 1902. *Brooklyn* then served with the European Squadron from June 1903 through February 1904. Three months later, as the new South Atlantic Squadron flagship, *Brooklyn* led three US

gunboats to Tangier in a naval show-of-force during the farcical Perdicaris Affair. The following year, *Brooklyn* steamed for Cherbourg, France to receive the disinterred remains of American Revolutionary War naval hero John Paul Jones. *Brooklyn* then returned to the United States, where on July 23, 1905, Jones' remains were ceremoniously re-interred in a new vault at the US Naval Academy in Annapolis, Maryland.

By March 1905, as its first new Pennsylvania-class cruisers began arriving, the USN upgraded the North Atlantic Squadron to the North Atlantic Fleet, composed of the First Squadron (battleships), Second Squadron (cruisers), Third Squadron (cruisers and gunboats), and Coast Squadron (coast defense battleships and monitors). By October 1905, *Pennsylvania*, *Colorado*, *West Virginia*, and *Maryland* comprised a cruiser division on the US East Coast. However, the division would transfer to the Asiatic in September 1906.

By 1907 the USN would consolidate its North Atlantic, South Atlantic, and European squadrons into a single Virginia-based Atlantic Fleet – the Great White Fleet. In December the Great White Fleet's 16 battleships, six destroyers, and five auxiliaries departed on their epic 15-month global circumnavigation. No armored cruisers accompanied them – the USN had placed *Brooklyn* and *New York* in ordinary, and had already deployed its eight Pennsylvania- and Tennessee-class cruisers to the West Coast.

The USN's final two armored cruisers, *North Carolina* and *Montana*, became operational in 1908 on the US East Coast. Accompanied by battleships *New Hampshire*, *Mississippi*, and *Idaho*, they would make a mid-Atlantic rendezvous with the returning Great White Fleet in February 1909. Together the 19 battleships and two armored cruisers made a triumphant homecoming into Hampton Roads on February 22, George Washington's birthday. From April through July, *Montana* and *North Carolina* deployed to the Levant in response to the Adana Massacre in Ottoman Turkey. The cruisers' mission was to protect American interests while also offering humanitarian assistance ashore.

"A Flock of Uncle Sam's Peace Doves at the Brooklyn Navy-Yard." So reads the original caption of this 1906 photograph. *West Virginia* is in the foreground, while *Maryland* is to the left. *Colorado* and *Pennsylvania* are in the background, along with battleships *Indiana* and *Alabama*. The armored cruisers are preparing to deploy to the Asiatic Station. (LOC LC-USZ62-66021)

Bluejackets and marines of a *Washington* landing party at Haiti, 1915. They are likely posing for the camera. Forced to wear their standard shipboard uniforms when fighting ashore, sailors often dyed their normal tropical whites khaki by boiling them in vats of coffee; they appear to be wearing coffee-dyed uniforms here. (Getty Images 514689594)

By 1912 the United States had begun heavily intervening in the so-called "Banana Wars" of Latin America. No US armored cruisers participated in the April 1914 intervention in Veracruz, Mexico, although the following month *Montana* returned the bodies of the American dead back to the United States. In July 1915, *Washington* would land marines and its own naval infantry at Port-au-Prince, Haiti to restore order there.

The *Memphis* disaster, August 29, 1916

On May 21, 1916, *Tennessee* steamed from Philadelphia for Santo Domingo, Dominican Republic to intervene in the ongoing Dominican crisis. Four days later, while *Tennessee* was underway, the USN renamed the ship *Memphis*. For the following three months *Memphis* cruised between Santo Domingo and Port-au-Prince, Haiti. Commanding *Memphis* was Captain Edward Beach, while Rear Admiral Charles Pond rode her as his flagship.

Memphis' Dominican service was uneventful until August 29. *Memphis* and gunboat *Castine* (PG-6) were then moored at Santo Domingo, already well-known to USN officers as a poor and dangerous anchorage. Santo Domingo was fairly exposed to weather, its water was often rough, and the anchorage itself was rocky and restricted. *Memphis* was anchored near the mouth of the Ozama Rio in nine fathoms (55ft) of water on a known submarine shelf or ledge so narrow that, within a few yards, the 10-fathom (60ft) curve dropped off to 100 fathoms (600ft).

Because of the known danger, *Memphis* typically expected to get underway within 45 minutes, but this usually required six of *Memphis*' 16 boilers to be lit. *Memphis*' skipper, Captain Beach, had wanted to keep at least four boilers lit, but Rear Admiral Pond, embarked aboard *Memphis* but ashore on August 29, had for budgetary reasons ordered only two boilers be kept lit, with four more ready to light.

Beginning at 1300hrs, *Memphis* sent the day's first recreation boat ashore, as usual, with further boats following at regular intervals. Seas were rough, but not unusually so. Then, around 1535hrs, *Memphis*' Captain Beach noticed a severe swell developing, despite near perfect meteorological conditions. Beach ordered *Memphis* to get underway, but sea spray was already entering the engine room through *Memphis*' ventilators and causing problems raising steam. *Memphis* was now rolling heavily in estimated 40ft waves and her decks had become awash.

Just after 1600hrs, "an immense wave or swell" was seen approaching. Upon reaching *Memphis* the swell's face "became very steep" but *Memphis* rode over it. However, 15 minutes earlier a launch had been sent to retrieve the party ashore. After heading back to *Memphis*, the launch was about 500yds from the cruiser when the first swell hit just after 1600hrs, the swell having already passed *Memphis*. At 1605hrs the second swell arrived, throwing the boat "end over end" according to an eyewitness and sinking it. Thirty-two of the 38 men aboard

Struggling to reach the open sea, the 212ft long, 1,177-ton gunboat *Castine* is visibly dwarfed by huge, breaking waves off Santo Domingo on August 29, 1916. This photograph was probably taken by *Memphis* early during the event, when she was still anchored seawards of *Castine* and before *Memphis* herself was driven ashore. Cheered heartily by *Memphis* sailors, at 1730hrs *Castine* did finally stagger to relative safety, the struggle to escape the apocalyptic anchorage having taken almost 90 minutes. *Castine* had lost three men dead. (NH 101130)

perished, either by drowning or being smashed into the shoreline. Of the six men who survived, several were thrown safely into nearby Fort Ozama, situated atop a cliff 40ft above sea level.

According to *Memphis'* Lieutenant-Commander Thomas Withers, "It is impossible for me to describe the astounding abruptness of the emergency." Wave after wave now followed every 30 seconds. Gunboat *Castine* struggled to head to sea, where it appeared to vanish time and again in the oncoming waves' troughs. According to Withers, these "enormous seas ... were *unaccompanied by any wind whatsoever*."

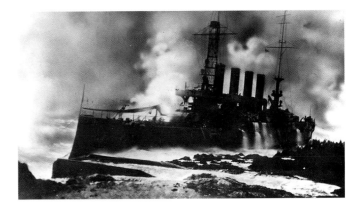

Armored cruiser *Memphis* is seen on the afternoon or evening of August 29, 1916, after heavy swells and a freak wave have run it hard aground at Santo Domingo, Dominican Republic. The photograph is authentic but appears to have been re-touched. *Memphis* would never return to service. (NH 65672)

Five minutes later, at 1610hrs, *Memphis'* log reports "the seas were breaking across our decks." By 1615hrs Lieutenant-Commander Withers reported that *Memphis* was dragging its anchor and striking the sea bottom in the trough of every wave. Captain Beach closed *Memphis'* watertight doors, but attempts to jettison *Memphis'* remaining anchor failed. By 1620hrs, *Memphis* began to drag along the seafloor, with the "steep front of each wave [acting] as an inclined plane" that forced *Memphis* a couple of hundred feet closer to shore. After another five minutes *Memphis* was rolling 60–70 degrees in the swells' troughs, so severely that seawater began pouring into intakes 50ft above the waterline, flooding the dynamo room, and extinguishing the boilers and any chance for *Memphis* to escape. As power failed, all of the cruiser's lights went out.

At 1635hrs *Memphis'* men observed a massive, strangely ocher wave on the horizon heading towards them. At around 1640hrs, this final mountainous wave, estimated at up to 100ft high, delivered the reeling cruiser its *coup de grâce*. The breaking rogue wave slammed into *Memphis* with tremendous power, smashing the 14,500-ton cruiser into the rocky seafloor so violently that most men were thrown to the deck and heavy equipment and ready ammunition throughout the ship began to tear loose and crash down, with "below decks [becoming] a death trap."

Still hammered by waves, by 1650hrs *Memphis* had been thrown into its final resting place in a mere 15ft of water and just 40ft from the beach cliffs. After some difficulty, several lines were rigged and, helped by marines and natives ashore, men began to be evacuated via breeches buoy. Some 750 crew were rescued by 2050hrs, including many badly injured. *Memphis'* companion, gunboat *Castine*, ultimately escaped the harbor, losing three dead.

Memphis was utterly destroyed. The six-hour ordeal ultimately killed 43 US sailors and severely injured 204. However, the subsequent December 1916 court martial censured *Memphis'* Captain Beach lightly, believing the event largely out of Beach's control. His career intact, Beach would later command battleship *New York* in 1918, while his son would make a submerged circumnavigation of the Earth as skipper of nuclear submarine *Triton*. The USN salvaged what heavy equipment it could from *Memphis*. The wreck itself was finally scrapped in 1937. Modern analysis suggests multiple hurricanes hundreds of miles away had combined with Santo

Domingo's unfavorable underwater topography to produce the unusually severe wave phenomenon. *Memphis* remains the largest active US warship destroyed at sea by natural disaster.

Pennsylvania-class armored cruiser *Maryland* in the South China Sea, March 6, 1907. She was part of an armored cruiser division that had temporarily redeployed to the Asiatic to replace US battleships. After the Russo-Japanese War, the USN began to reduce its presence in Asia. In a few months the armored cruisers would be withdrawn to the US West Coast. (NH 83807)

Asiatic and Pacific 1899–1917

In December 1899 *Brooklyn* arrived at Manila Bay, becoming the new Asiatic Squadron flagship and fighting in the 1899–1902 Filipino-American War. Within weeks *Brooklyn*'s marine detachment would help rescue 522 Spanish prisoners-of-war being held by Filipino insurgents. Months later, *Brooklyn*'s marine contingent participated in the relief of the international delegation during the 1900 Boxer Rebellion. By May, *New York* had also reached the Philippines for counter-insurgency operations.

By October 1903 both *Brooklyn* and *New York* had been detached from the Asiatic, although battleships *Oregon*, *Kentucky*, *Wisconsin*, and *Ohio* variously deployed there for several more years. However, after the 1904–05 Russo-Japanese War, it was clear the large, fast, and modern

G **USS *MEMPHIS* STRUCK BY FATAL 100FT ROGUE WAVE WHILE ANCHORED AT SANTO DOMINGO, DOMINICAN REPUBLIC, AUGUST 29, 1916**

On August 29, 1916, armored cruiser *Memphis* (ex-*Tennessee*) found herself the tragic victim of one of the most bizarre episodes in USN history. Moored hundreds of yards offshore of Santo Domingo, Dominican Republic, at 1535hrs *Memphis* began to be hit by a series of increasingly powerful swells and breakers. Alarmed, *Memphis*' Captain Beach ordered steam raised in order to escape the harbor; his engineers reported that despite considerable flooding they would have sufficient pressure to power the engines within an hour.

At 1635hrs, lookouts noticed an immense 100ft wave approaching on the horizon. As the freak wave closed on *Memphis*, the shallower seafloor caused it to slow in speed and rise in height. A huge trough preceded the monster wave for 300ft, while its waveform "appeared to consist of three distinct steps, each separated by a large plateau." The wave itself was a visibly ocher color, as it "could be seen churning sediments of sand and mud from the sea bottom." Captain Beach desperately attempted to turn *Memphis* into the wave by ordering *Memphis*' port engine full ahead and starboard engine full reverse, but at only 90psi there was simply not enough steam pressure to fully turn *Memphis* into the oncoming wave. *Memphis* would be struck broadside, the worst possible position.

Once the wave reached a seafloor depth of 90ft, at 1640hrs, the wave's peaking crest began to break some 30–40ft above the level of *Memphis*' bridge. By now the wave's potential energy had fully transformed into kinetic energy, throwing a vast amount of water forward at a speed of 25–30mph and causing "the huge wave [to break] thunderously upon the *Memphis*, completely engulfing it." *Memphis* rolled hard to port, smashing into the seafloor violently but righted herself, refusing to capsize. Below decks, *Memphis*' boilers exploded while the rocky seafloor mangled and tore *Memphis*' hull. Two men trying to release *Memphis*' second anchor were thrown overboard. Another eight were scalded to death by the erupting boilers. Within minutes the ruined *Memphis* had been pushed into the rocky Santo Domingo coast, stranding her and allowing her captain to order her abandoned. The long and dangerous rescue operation was completed by evening, with much help provided by locals.

In September 1916, the official US Navy inquiry called the inexplicable phenomenon both a "tsunami" and a "seismic storm," but these vague and unsupported terms do not fit the conditions observed, especially as no seismic event in the region had been recorded for months. Modern oceanographic science now suggests the random breakers and fatal freak wave was a "meteotsunami" that had been produced days earlier by three hurricanes hundreds of miles away. More critically, if *Memphis* had been anchored in 100ft of water instead of 55ft, she would have easily ridden over the swells before they broke, including the 100ft rogue wave.

South Dakota seen stern-on at Mare Island Drydock #2, March 15, 1910. Earlier that day *South Dakota* had become the first ship to enter the new drydock. Like most US armored cruisers, *South Dakota* had a long career in the Pacific. In October 1919 *South Dakota* began a seven-year career as the Asiatic Fleet flagship, was renamed *Huron* in 1920, and was finally decommissioned in June 1927. (US Navy)

The beached St. Louis-class semi-armored cruiser *Milwaukee* lies helpless off Eureka, California on January 13, 1917. The crew is being rowed ashore. *Milwaukee* had run aground in the dark earlier that morning while attempting to help refloat a submarine that had also run aground. Later attempts to salvage the cruiser failed, and by November 1918 *Milwaukee's* wreck had broken in two. (NH 46156)

Imperial Japanese Navy was more powerful than any detached battleship division the USN was willing to risk overseas. The USN's slow and outnumbered Asia-based battleships were not expected to survive a surprise offensive by the locally superior IJN, and in September 1906 the USN recalled its last battleships to North America. In contrast, US armored cruisers were too fast to easily run down, they could engage in aggressive commerce raiding after war broke out, and (one suspects) they were ultimately considered more expendable than battleships. Therefore, in late 1906 the USN temporarily transferred *Pennsylvania*, *West Virginia*, *Maryland*, and *Colorado* to the Far East to replace the recently departed battleships.

In April 1907 the USN combined the Asiatic Fleet and Pacific Squadron into a single Pacific Fleet, with the armored cruisers *Pennsylvania*, *West Virginia*, *Maryland*, and *Colorado* becoming the Pacific Fleet's First Division, and *California*, *South Dakota*, *Washington*, and *Tennessee* the Second Division. Together the two divisions comprised the Pacific Fleet's powerful First Squadron of eight modern armored cruisers, all based in California. Meanwhile, by 1907 all three St. Louis-class semi-armored cruisers, protected cruiser *Albany*, and gunboat *Yorktown* had been consolidated on the West Coast. Together they comprised the new Pacific Fleet's Second Squadron.

In January 1910 the USN again reorganized its commands, dividing the single, unified Pacific Fleet into separate Asiatic and Pacific Fleets. *New York* returned to the Far East that August for flagship duty. As the renamed *Saratoga*, it would cruise China and the Philippines until relieved by *Brooklyn* in February 1916.

By 1912, the United States was militarily intervening in Latin America on both Atlantic and Pacific coasts. In August 1912, a Pacific squadron with *California* as flagship helped crush a revolt in Nicaragua, with *California* and *Colorado* contributing a major landing force.

Milwaukee's demise, January 1917

In December 1916, submarines USS *H-1*, *H-2*, *H-3*, and their tender, monitor USS *Cheyenne*, were steaming along the US West Coast, making a routine visit to the Northern California port of Eureka. The coastline here is often foggy, and on December 14 *H-3* ran aground on Samoa Beach, near the mouth of Eureka's Humboldt Bay. Tug USS *Iroquois* and Coast Guard cutter *McCulloch* shortly arrived to help *Cheyenne* pull *H-3* free, but the subsequent December 19 effort failed.

The USN then received two civilian offers to salvage the submarine. The first contractor's proposal, by the West Coast's largest marine salvage firm, was rejected for being too expensive at $150,000. The second – by Mercer-Fraser, a local Eureka lumber company – was an $18,000 bid to use logs and drag *H-3* nearly a mile over the sandbar and into Humboldt Bay to be refloated.

The USN rejected this bid for supposedly being unrealistic. Despite lacking appropriate experience or equipment, the USN elected to try and salvage *H-3* itself.

The Pacific Fleet's Coast Torpedo Force flagship, semi-armored cruiser *Milwaukee*, joined *Cheyenne*, *Iroquois*, and *McCulloch* at Samoa Beach on January 7, 1917, to reinforce USN salvage operations. At over 21,000hp, *Milwaukee* had much more powerful engines than her companions. However, in addition to the fog, Eureka's currents are notoriously strong and unpredictable.

By evening January 12, the combined towing formation was in place, but in low visibility and high seas *Cheyenne*'s stabilizing line to *Milwaukee*'s starboard bows snapped. Out of control, *Iroquois* had to cut her own line to *Milwaukee*, leaving the cruiser free to swing in the strong current while still anchored to *H-3* on shore. *Milwaukee*'s crew attempted to cut this last line by hacksaw, but the heavy cable proved too robust. In the dark, the current inevitably dragged *Milwaukee* towards shore. By 0400hrs, January 13, *Milwaukee* had come hard aground parallel to the beach. As *Milwaukee* rolled incessantly in the heavy, relentless surf her hull predictably failed. Flooding seawater extinguished *Milwaukee*'s boilers and disabled her machinery. *Milwaukee* was now clearly doomed, and her 450-man crew urgently needed rescue before the cruiser broke up catastrophically.

By late morning the fog had lifted and a crowd of locals began congregating onshore, both to gawk and to help. A line was rigged from *Milwaukee* to shore, upon which the first men were evacuated via precarious breeches buoy. Eventually, two local-manned boats helped pull men off as the surf gradually lessened. By evening all crew were safely ashore with only a few injuries. After salvage attempts failed, *Milwaukee* was dismantled in place and decommissioned in March 1917, its hulk abandoned to the elements.

Ironically, that April, Eureka's Mercer-Fraser would recover *H-3* by dragging the submarine over the sand and into Humboldt Bay – the company's original $18,000 proposal which the USN had rejected back in December. In between, the USN had suffered a national public relations disaster and had lost a $2.8 million cruiser. Over the decades, *Milwaukee*'s remaining hulk essentially sank into the quicksand; up to two-thirds of *Milwaukee*'s hull still lies off Samoa Beach, buried out of sight beneath the shallow seafloor. Indeed, as of 2020, traces of *Milwaukee*'s ruins were still visible at extreme low tide.

Milwaukee's forecastle seen on April 29, 1919, over two years after she foundered off Eureka, California. Marine growth is visible on the wooden deck, and the forward 6in guns have been removed. The view is from *Milwaukee*'s bridge and was photographed by Emma B. Freeman of Eureka. (NH 46162)

Aviation 1911–17

On November 4, 1910, Eugene Ely, a stunt pilot employed by Glenn Curtiss, took off from the anchored protected cruiser *Birmingham* and landed ashore in Virginia – the first launch of an aircraft from a ship in history. Urged by Ely and Curtiss, the USN would commence a flurry of ship-based aviation-related experiments on the West Coast. On January 4, 1911, engineers at California's Mare Island Navy Yard began modifying armored cruiser *Pennsylvania* into an experimental aviation ship, building an elevated 130ft

Eugene Ely lands successfully on *Pennsylvania*'s temporary flight deck, January 11, 1918. Ely's ingenious arrestor gear system is visible, plus the two inner guide rails and the outer canvas awnings. The landing was something of a public spectacle and attracted thousands of spectators both afloat on ships in the bay and standing along the shore. (NH 82737)

In June 1916 *North Carolina*'s original catapult was removed and an improved *Huntington*-style catapult was installed. It consisted of a 103ft-long track suspended 13ft above the quarterdeck, which allowed it to clear *North Carolina*'s after 10in turret. The portside feeder track is also visible. (US Navy and Marine Corps Museum/Naval Aviation Museum, Photo No.2008.104.001.178)

long, 32ft wide landing platform over *Pennsylvania*'s stern. To arrest a landing plane, Ely's team devised an ingenious solution. Ropes with sandbags at each end would be laid perpendicularly across *Pennsylvania*'s landing platform. A hook added to Ely's plane's tail would then grab the sandbag-weighted ropes, safely dragging Ely to a stop.

At 1045hrs on the morning of January 18, 1911, Eugene Ely lifted off from San Bruno, California's Tanforan Racetrack in a Curtiss Model D pusher biplane and headed for *Pennsylvania*, anchored off Hunter's Point in San Francisco Bay. *Pennsylvania*'s Captain Charles F. Pond, anticipating future carrier methods, had argued that *Pennsylvania* should land Ely in the open sea, steaming into a headwind at 10–20 knots. Ely, however, insisted *Pennsylvania* be at anchor.

About 75ft from *Pennsylvania*, Ely cut his engine. The tailwind carried him to the landing deck for a centerline landing at 40mph. Ely overflew the first 11 arrestor ropes but caught the next 11 and came to a stop. Captain Pond recorded: "Nothing [was] damaged, and not a bolt or brace started, and Ely [was] the coolest man aboard." It was the first time an airplane had ever landed aboard a ship. Ely was immediately congratulated by his waiting wife and given a celebratory lunch in *Pennsylvania*'s mess. An hour later Ely lifted off from the same *Pennsylvania* platform he had just landed on and flew back to the Tanforan Racetrack.

Six days later, on January 24, 1911 Lieutenant John Rodgers lifted off in a manned kite balloon from *Pennsylvania*, now anchored in the Santa Barbara Channel. Rodgers' feat proved history's second ever balloon ascent from a ship (the first was in 1861).

Then on February 17, 1911, Glenn Curtiss landed his modified Model D hydroaeroplane (seaplane) alongside *Pennsylvania* in San Diego harbor. *Pennsylvania* then hoisted Curtiss and his plane aboard. Thirty minutes later *Pennsylvania* lowered Curtiss and his hydroaeroplane back into the water, and Curtiss took off again. It was Curtiss' feat, more than the better-celebrated Ely episodes, that finally sold the USN on naval aviation.

In September 1915, the USN modified armored cruiser *North Carolina* with a stern-mounted catapult. On November 5, Lieutenant-Commander Henry Mustin launched his flying boat *AB-2* from *North Carolina*, anchored in Pensacola. It was not only history's first catapult launch from a commissioned warship, but also the first launch of an aircraft from a ship that was underway.

In March 1916, the USN decommissioned *Washington* for overhaul. She was fitted with an aircraft catapult and recommissioned as *Seattle* on November 9, 1916. *Seattle* shortly

redeployed to Cuban waters, where she launched the first aerial missions from a ship at sea to observe Cuban insurgent movements. While off Cuba, *Seattle* fitted a hydroaeroplane with an airborne radio, another naval aviation first.

By early 1917, at Mare Island, *Huntington* (ex-*West Virginia*) had become the third US armored cruiser fitted with specialized aircraft handling equipment, including a catapult. By June 7, 1917, *Huntington* had arrived at Pensacola, Florida and taken aboard Lieutenant Junior-Grade Marc Mitscher's air group of seven pilots, 26 enlisted men, four Thomas-Morse pontoon biplanes, and several manned kite balloons.

The following day, *Huntington* began aviation experiments to develop aerial ASW techniques against German U-boats. *Huntington*'s clueless but enthusiastic skipper, Captain Samuel Robeson, suggested a skeptical Mitscher try launching from one of *Huntington*'s swung-out airplane derricks while *Huntington* was underway. With the pontoons digging into the water, *Huntington* predictably dragged Mitscher's plane until it slammed into *Huntington*'s hull, nearly killing Mitscher. The experiment was not repeated.

World War I 1917–18
On April 6, 1917, the United States declared war on Imperial Germany. There were then three armored cruisers and one semi-armored cruiser stationed in the Atlantic (*Montana*, *North Carolina*, *Seattle*, and *Charleston*), and six armored cruisers and one semi-armored cruiser stationed in the Pacific (*South Dakota*, *Huntington*, *Frederick*, *San Diego*, *Pueblo*, *Saratoga*, and *St. Louis*). Within days, the first Pacific Fleet cruisers, *South Dakota* and *St. Louis*, had transferred to the Atlantic. After patrolling the eastern Pacific, the last Pacific Fleet armored cruiser, *Saratoga*, transited the Panama Canal in November 1917. *Saratoga* brought the Atlantic Fleet to nine armored cruisers and two semi-armored cruisers; *Brooklyn* and *Pittsburgh* remained on the Asiatic station.

To defeat Germany, the United States began raising a huge new US field army called the American Expeditionary Force (AEF). Safely transporting the AEF to France became the USN's primary wartime mission. On May 23, 1917, the USN appointed Rear Admiral Albert Gleaves to lead transatlantic convoy operations as commander of the newly established Cruiser and Transport Force. Under Gleaves the Cruiser and Transport Force would eventually reach 75 fast merchantmen and liners, divided into two divisions. The escorts were themselves divided into two squadrons deploying from New York, Newport News, and Halifax, with most armored cruisers in the First Squadron. Typically, the cruisers escorted their charges across the Atlantic, rendezvoused with new escorts in European waters, and then turned around and steamed back to North America. Such long-range missions required up to 1,000 tons of additional coal to be stowed on deck per round-trip.

In June 1917, Gleaves' flagship *Seattle* and semi-armored cruisers *St. Louis* and *Charleston* helped successfully escort the

Armored cruiser *Huntington* (ex-*West Virginia*) deploys a kite balloon off Pensacola, June 23, 1917. The US Navy was more enthusiastic about naval aviation in this era than is generally reported. However, the US armored cruisers' contribution is often forgotten compared to the later flush-decked aircraft carrier. (US Navy and Marine Corps Museum/ Naval Aviation Museum, Photo No.1988.120.001.001)

A heavy layer of frozen sea spray coats the forward 8in/40 guns of Pennsylvania-class cruiser USS *Frederick* (ex-*Maryland*) in March 1918. Based out of Halifax, Nova Scotia, *Frederick* was part of a four-cruiser division escorting convoys in the bitterly cold North Atlantic. (NH 50357)

AEF's first transatlantic convoy to France, although on June 22 a U-boat's torpedo salvo just missed *Seattle* by 50yds.

On September 17, 1917, armored cruiser *Huntington* found herself underway in the North Atlantic as Convoy Group 7 flagship. All seaplanes had been stowed because they were unrecoverable in U-boat infested waters, leaving only the kite balloons operational. However, while streaming a manned balloon aft at 400ft, *Huntington* inevitably found itself battered by a North Atlantic squall. *Huntington*'s violent motions eventually knocked balloon pilot Lieutenant J. G. Hoyt unconscious. Moments later Hoyt's balloon crashed into the sea, its tangled wreckage now dragged in *Huntington*'s wake.

Huntington's Captain Samuel Robeson repeatedly ordered Lieutenant Marc Mitscher to cut the mooring cable, casting the balloon adrift and certainly killing Hoyt, but Mitscher adamantly refused. Robeson finally ordered *Huntington*'s engines stopped, and Ship's Fitter First Class Patrick McGunigal, securing a lifeline around himself, dove into the sea and recovered the unconscious Hoyt from the submerged and tangled balloon basket. For courageously saving Hoyt's life McGunigal was awarded World War I's first Medal of Honor. The USN unsurprisingly removed *Huntington*'s aircraft and aviation equipment the following month.

Late on June 25, 1918, *Saratoga*, now renamed *Rochester*, sighted a U-boat while leading a moonlit, eastbound North Atlantic convoy. As *Rochester* turned to ram, the U-boat dove and fired a torpedo that missed *Rochester*'s bow by 30yds, instead hitting and sinking merchantman *Atlantian*. Within a few hours, a surfaced U-boat torpedoed a second merchantman. *Rochester* duly counterattacked but again the U-boat submerged and escaped.

The sinking of *San Diego*, July 19, 1918

Only seven German U-boats had the endurance to potentially operate off the US East Coast. The USN tracked them closely, and on June 14, 1918, Kapitänleutnant Richard Feldt's *U-156* departed Kiel for North America. While en route to lay mines off New York, *U-156* sank one British and two Norwegian merchantmen. For the next several months, *U-156* would be the only German U-boat operating in North American waters.

On July 19, 1918, Captain Harley Christy's armored cruiser *San Diego* was underway from Portsmouth, New Hampshire, to reinforce a convoy waiting in Brooklyn. *San Diego* was steaming west-southwest at 15 knots, parallel to Fire Island (a Long Island barrier island) which was about ten miles to starboard. The cruiser was zigzagging in smooth seas; visibility was six miles. By late morning *San Diego*

Armored cruiser USS *Huntington* (ex-*West Virginia*) viewed in 1918 during transatlantic convoy operations. She is in dazzle camouflage and no longer retains her aviation equipment. *Huntington*, *North Carolina*, and *Frederick* are all known to have received dazzle paint jobs during World War I. (NH 41797)

had rounded the Fire Island lightship and was 60 miles from its destination.

Suddenly at 1105hrs an explosion erupted well below the waterline on *San Diego*'s port side. Assuming *San Diego* had been hit by a torpedo, Christy immediately sounded submarine defense quarters, closing all watertight doors. Christy then ordered *San Diego*'s gunners to fire at anything that might be a periscope, while turning hard north for shore and ordering engines full ahead in hopes of beaching in shallow water; at best speed Fire Island's south shoreline was 30 minutes away. *San Diego* was unable to call for help, as the shock wave had knocked out her wireless. Unfortunately, the initial explosion had also pierced *San Diego*'s hull at the port engine room, mangling internal watertight integrity enough to let water pour into the No. 8 fireroom, causing a 17.5-degree list to port. Water progressively flooded *San Diego*'s engineering spaces, causing the cruiser to lose all power. As *San Diego* lost headway and succumbed to port, the sea began rushing in through the opening for the No. 10 6in gun; although the gun itself had long been removed, its hull opening had never been plated over. *San Diego*'s gun deck quickly flooded, sealing the cruiser's fate.

Ten minutes after the explosion Christy gave the order to abandon ship. However, the gun crews were ordered to keep shooting as long as possible. They fired 30 rounds into the sea before *San Diego*'s increasing list made the guns inoperable. Meanwhile, *San Diego*'s men evacuated in an orderly fashion into life rafts and small boats, with Christy the last to leave. When Christy's crew observed their captain safely evacuate the ship, they spontaneously erupted into cheers from their lifeboats, and began singing *The Star-Spangled Banner*.

The cruiser rolled over, floated upside-down for one minute, and then sank at 1125hrs, 20 minutes after the explosion. *San Diego* had foundered eight miles south of Fire Island in water 65–115ft deep. She had missed making Brooklyn by four hours. Navigating a dinghy to Long Island, *San Diego*'s Lieutenant C. J. Bright sent wireless messages to Brooklyn and nearby ships announcing the situation. Steamers *Malden*, *Bussan*, and *E. P. Jones* shortly arrived to pick up *San Diego*'s survivors. Only six men had died out of *San Diego*'s crew of 1,186.

San Diego had just become the only large US warship sunk in World War I due to enemy action. Exactly who and what had sunk her was at first a mystery. However, on August 2, Feldt's rampaging *U-156* destroyed the Canadian schooner *Dornfontein* and took its crew prisoner for five hours. While hosting the Canadians, the U-boat officers claimed to have laid the mine that had sunk *San Diego*. Feldt then released *Dornfontein*'s crew, allowing them to row safely to the New Brunswick shoreline. By August 26, Feldt's *U-156* had sunk 34 ships totaling 33,582 tons, and even shelled a Massachusetts village. However, while returning to Germany, *U-156*'s own end came unexpectedly and with bitter irony. On September 25, 1918, *U-156* struck an American-laid naval mine in the North Sea and sank without survivors.

The Sinking of USS San Diego, a 1920 watercolor by Francis Muller, depicts *San Diego* succumbing off Fire Island, New York on July 19, 1918. It had just struck a naval mine laid days earlier by German U-boat *U-156*. *San Diego*'s lifeboats can be seen rowing away from the sinking. (NH 55012-KN)

For its 1926–31 Asiatic service *Pittsburgh* received a major overhaul, including an enclosed bridge, a modern new fire control system, and the removal of her 6in/50 guns, eight boilers, and foremost funnel. *Pittsburgh* nevertheless retained a 20-knot top speed. (NH 720)

North Carolina gets underway off the Pensacola naval station in 1916. Flying boat *AB-3* can be seen on the new stern catapult, possibly getting ready to launch. The armored cruisers were instrumental in the development of shipboard US naval aviation, but World War I forced the USN to abandon their experimental aviation mission. All armored cruisers' aviation equipment was removed in late 1917 or early 1918. (US Navy and Marine Corps Museum/Naval Aviation Museum, Photo No.2008.104.001.183)

Twilight careers 1918–46

World War I ended in November 1918, leaving 2.1 million AEF troops stranded in Europe. A massive, improvised troop lift immediately began taking them home. Of the surviving Big Ten cruisers, all but *Pittsburgh* helped repatriate doughboys, with six cruisers making six round-trips each and *South Dakota* making two. *Huntington* brought the most home, at 11,913 troops. The seven Big Ten cruisers combined for 60,689 doughboys returned in 38 round-trips, an average of 1,597 per voyage. Additionally, *Rochester* (ex-*New York*) completed a single round-trip in early 1919, ferrying 300 doughboys. Semi-armored cruisers *St. Louis* and *Charleston* combined for 12 round-trips, bringing home an additional 16,137 American personnel.

In July 1918, *Brooklyn* had deployed to the Siberian port of Vladivostok to intervene in the ongoing Russian Civil War. For several months *Brooklyn* deployed a marine detachment ashore as part of a major multinational expedition to safeguard Allied war materiel against Bolshevik capture. However, by summer 1919, the Bolsheviks had begun routing the Allied-supported White Russian forces. By January 1920, armored cruiser *South Dakota* would moor at Vladivostok to cover the evacuation of the American expeditionary force. The morning of January 31, *South Dakota* and her naval infantry fell under attack by Bolshevik troops penetrating the city. Over several days *South Dakota*'s infantry successfully repulsed the Bolsheviks in the midst of a raging -40°F blizzard, restoring the situation. By May 1920 the American evacuation had been completed and *South Dakota* departed Vladivostok.

The 1930 London Naval Conference sealed the fate of the long obsolete armored and semi-armored cruisers, and all but three would be disposed of before 1931. Among the brief survivors was *Pittsburgh* (ex-*Pennsylvania*), which in 1926 had been designated the Asiatic Fleet flagship. *Pittsburgh* reached China in December 1926 and began landing marines at Shanghai to protect Americans during the ongoing Chinese civil war. After five years' Asiatic duty, *Pittsburgh* was struck in 1931.

After three years of intervening in Latin America, *Rochester* (ex-*New York*) became the new Asiatic Fleet flagship in 1932. Twelve months later, on April 29, 1933, *Rochester* was permanently decommissioned in Manila Bay, making the 40-year-old former *New York* both the first and the last active US armored cruiser. She was then permanently moored at Olangapo in Subic Bay. As an unclassified hulk, ex-*Rochester* remained at Olangapo until December 24, 1941, when she was scuttled to avoid capture by the Japanese.

Rochester was outlived in formal commission only by *Seattle* (ex-*Washington*), which had served as the US Fleet flagship between 1923 and 1927.

However, in 1931 *Seattle* was reclassified as a receiving ship and permanently moored in New York, serving in this capacity through World War II. *Seattle* was finally decommissioned in June 1946, the last of the US armored cruisers.

CONCLUSION

Although they were expensive and controversial, US armored cruisers were among the finest of their type in the world. American armored cruisers were fast, seaworthy, and heavily armed command ships that served their country well. They possessed none of the inexplicable flaws and shaky design concepts that plagued the earliest US battleships.

As high-speed, well-armed flagships of the US Atlantic Fleet's two battle squadrons, *New York* and *Brooklyn* played vital roles in the 1898 Spanish-American War. US armored cruisers' size and speed additionally made them natural testbeds for new technology, with *Pennsylvania*, *North Carolina*, *Seattle*, and *Huntington* all making significant contributions to the development of US naval aviation. Moreover, the Big Ten cruisers were among the first warships legitimately reaching towards the mythical "fast battleship" dream that married cruiser speed with battleship power – a dream the USN would finally realize with the 1943 Iowa-class battleships.

SELECT BIBLIOGRAPHY

Alden, Commander John T., *The American Steel Navy*, Naval Institute Press (2008)

Chadwick, Captain F. E., "The *New York* at Santiago. By her Commander," *The Century Quarterly*, Vol. 58 (1899)

Cook, Captain Francis A., "The *Brooklyn* at Santiago. By her Commander," *The Century Quarterly*, Vol. 58 (1899)

Friedman, Norman, *U.S. Cruisers: An Illustrated Design History*, Naval Institute Press (1984)

Jampoler, Andrew C. A., "The Short Life and Hard Times of an Armored Cruiser," *Naval History Magazine*, Vol. 30, No. 4, August 2016

Leeke, Jim, *Manila and Santiago: The New Steel Navy in the Spanish-American War*, Naval Institute Press (2009)

McCue, Michael Westaway, "The U-Boat That Threatened America," *American History Magazine*, February 2002

Musicant, Ivan, *U.S. Armored Cruisers: A Design and Operational History*, Naval Institute Press (1985)

Riggs, Ensign R. R., "The Question of Speed in Battleships," USNI *Proceedings*, Vol. 34 (1908)

Withers Jr., Lieutenant Commander Thomas, "The Wreck of the U.S.S. *Memphis*," USNI *Proceedings*, Vol. 44/7/185 (1918)

Young, James Rankin, *The Story of Our Wonderful Victories, Told by Dewey, Schley, Wheeler, and Other Heroes*, Philadelphia (1899)

https://www.history.navy.mil/

https://www.loc.gov/

https://www.spanamwar.com/

www.navsource.com

www.navweaps.com

INDEX

Page numbers in **bold** refer to illustrations and some caption locators are in brackets. Page numbers in *italic* refer to tables.